Sleeping Saints

Today's Christians need to wake up and cry aloud. They need to tear down and root up old philosophies that have caused the church to enter her own slumber land. While the church rests drowsily in a spiritual stupor, the lost world is running obliviously toward the pit of destruction. The door of opportunity to save the lost will soon be closed.

William Combs

©2011 Copyright Williams Combs
All Rights Reserved

ISBN-13: 978-0-615-48095-4

ISBN-10: 0-615-48095-0

Printed in the United States of America

Cover Credits: Photos Shutterstock

Table of Contents

Acknowledgements iv

Preface v

1 Holy Heartburn 1

2 Leaving the Savior Behind 17

3 Parable of the Sower, Seeds and Soils.......................... 35

4 Sleeping Saints:... 103

      Inner Preface.. 104

      1 Introduction to Sleeping Saints.............................. 107

      2 Sleeping During Preaching 121

      3 Sleeping During the Time of Transfiguration....... 137

      4 Sleeping During Prayer... 151

      5 Sleeping While the Lord Tarries His Return 165

5 Satisfying Man's Natural and Spiritual Needs for Body and Soul 183

    Part 1: Satisfying Man's Natural Needs for His Body 183

    Part 2: Satisfying Man's Spiritual Needs for His Soul...... 207

6 An Analogy of Spiritual Anemia.................................. 235

      Appendix: Sermon Outlines 300

Index 316

    Index of Scripture 317

    Author Index... 319

— ACKNOWLEDGEMENTS —

I would like to thank my Mother, Rosalie, and my grandparents, L.D. Martin, for making sure I attended church as a child. A special thanks goes to Francis McBride and family, who, one night, invited me to a revival meeting. That night I trusted Jesus Christ as my personal Savior. Double thanks should go to the unknown but not forgotten evangelist who preached that eventful evening.

All the faithful Sunday school teachers must be recognized for consistently planting and watering the seeds of God's love and grace through the years. Special thanks goes to all my seminary professors who made the Scriptures live as did all the pastors that I sat under. These men gave me the burning desire to continue in-depth study of the Word after graduation.

All the members of my former churches should be recognized that gave favorable responses to the messages you are about to read the first time around. No author should forget to recognize the person who finalized all the long hours of writing and rewriting, Lisa Monias, for her long hours of labor in layout and design of the book.

I am particular appreciative for Vera, my beloved wife of forty years, who has been my greatest supporter, prayer warrior, and critic. She was always available to add insight, corrective spelling, and spiritual perception line upon line.

A hardy thanks goes to the reader who is about to read these few pages. My prayer is that you will receive a blessing and that you might wish to share that blessing with another person.

— PREFACE —

The following messages you are about to read have been presented to several congregations. Since there was such a positive response to each message in regard to salvations, baptisms, and enlightenment of scriptures, and after prayer, I was led to believe that the same messages may be a blessing to you, your pastor, and/or your church.

Sermon preparation is an art similar to creating a painting. Some works of art require a few hours while others mandate weeks or months to complete. The casual onlooker does not realize paintings completed in a few minutes are actually the results of years of accumulated knowledge and countless throw a ways and practices. Likewise, each sermon a minister delivers is made up, if only in part, by the accumulation of both his current study and all the messages he has ever heard, read, or preached. Therefore, some of the illustrations included in the following messages may not be original but they were done in order to document another person's thoughts on the given subject. Any similarity to another's message must be the work of the Holy Spirit or derived from my personal notes over the last 35 years. Personal and intimate experiences have been shared with the hope that they may show the reader that he or she is not the only person to suffer such difficulty. I pray that the Spirit of Revival will fall upon a number of churches or individuals that are bold enough to use some of these thoughts.

The revised edition of *Sleeping Saints* was penned because enough material had come to mind afterward the first edition to warrant a makeover. The rewrite gave me the opportunity to further refine the original works. Two messages were replaced by ones more in tune with the overall thesis of the book. Pictures and art work were included in some instances to add clarity to the message being presented. An appendix of sermon outlines was added for each entry to serve as a springboard for the pastor or teacher who would like to adapt a particular message for his or her congregation or Sunday school class.

The Holy Heartburn came to mind while reading chapter 24 from the Gospel of Luke. The two traveler's heart burned within them as Jesus was sharing His word. The idea for *Leaving the Savior Behind* came while a visiting missionary friend stayed with us while he was on furlough. During our private devotions one night, he used the phrase, "leaving the Savior behind" from the Gospel of Luke, chapter two. I borrowed his phrase and developed a message with the same phrase. Several people rededicated their lives after hearing *Leaving the Savior Behind*. *The Parable of the*

Sower, Seeds and Soils was first written as a four-week Sunday school lesson while I was filling in for a staff member of a local church; but it can easily be preached in two or more sermons. (Pastors should never hurry through their messages or cut important content from the sermon just to finish at a certain time. The average sermon today lasts 10 to 15 minutes or less; whereas, pastors during my great-great grandfather's era, preached for more than an hour.) The parable of the soils is included in this series because of such an overwhelming response that was received from the Sunday school class. It seemed a number of Christians were experiencing problems in their spiritual walk; but no one had ever shared the fact that spiritual victory gradually comes in steps from personal labor and not necessarily from the supernatural prayers of others. A number of Christians identified the soil they represented (from the parable) due to the temptations and/or difficulties they were experiencing.

The five sermons that make up the *Sleeping Saints* series were developed after a pastoral friend referred to the modern church as a group of sleeping saints in his introduction to his message. The intent again was to preach a simple five-point message; but the Holy Spirit had other ideas. During the preparation too much support came forth for each scriptural text to adequately present it in a single message. A second preface page is included to introduce the series and to explain the origin of the original belief behind the five messages. The decision was made to entitle the entire book *Sleeping Saints* because of the way the other essays seemed to be in line to the same enigma of Christendom.

The Satisfying Man's Natural and Spiritual Needs for Body and Soul came from hours of counseling Christians and notes from my pastoral and psychology classes. Suggestions were made that Jesus could fulfill any and all of what a person ever will need to be a successful disciple. The seed of the message grew because the Spirit of God was allowed to freely guide the writer's hand. Thoughts and illustrations flooded my mind at such a rate that many of the points had to be written as mere side notes for later development. When the Holy Spirit is in control of sermon preparation, the message many times enters the pastor's mind faster than he can write. This could be the reason the final brief contained two divisions.

The concluding message, *An Analogy of Spiritual Anemia,* received its title after the faulting state of the modern church was discussed by a number of concerned Christians. Our focus settled on the general spiritual condition of the Christian sitting in the average American church. Even with the growing number of "mega churches" and the old fashion fire and brimstone preaching of country churches, (where the fire seems to be dying down) something has to be wrong or missing in the post-modern, 21st Century Christian. Our Christian communities, on a whole, are suffering a moral and spiritual melt-down. Salvation does not appear to have brought a change in the convert's life as promised by the Spirit of God. The Christian testifies that he or she is spiritual, but does not hold to the same unwavering beliefs in God the Father, the Bible, Jesus Christ, or the church as the preceding generations.

Each message has been drenched in prayer with the hope they will be a blessing to the reader and to his or her church.

Bibles references:

King James Version, The New Scofield Reference Bible. New York: Oxford University Press, 1967.

King James Version, The Open Bible –Expanded Edition. Nashville: Thomas Nelson Publishers, 1985.

The Amplified Bible. Grand Rapids, Mich.: Zondervan Bible Publishers, 1987.

— CHAPTER ONE —

Holy Heartburn

Preface: Before preaching this message I set a roll of *Rolaids*, a box of baking soda, and a bottle of *Pepto Bismol* on the Communion Table as an attention getter for the congregation. Since most everyone has experienced heartburn sometime in their life, I asked the audience what further remedies have they used to relieve heartburn. The response varied from one half a teaspoon of spirit of ammonia in Coke Cola to peppermint candy or a few drops of peppermint extract in a hot cup of water.

This morning I would like to speak about a different kind of heartburn – a spiritual heartburn.
Text: Luke 24: 13-35.
Selected verses: 13, 14, 32, 35: *And, behold, two of them*

Chapter One: Holy Heartburn

went that same day to a village called Emmaus, which was from Jerusalem [about] threescore furlongs. And they talked together of all these things which had happened. And they said one to another, Did not our heart burn within us, while he talked with us by the way, and while he opened to us the scriptures. And they told what things [were done] in the way, and how he was known of them in breaking of bread.

Heartburn or *Pyrosis* is sometimes called indigestion. Physicians refer to this condition as "gastric distress." The condition known as heartburn can rate from mild to severe. Heartburn derived its name from the symptom of a burning sensation in the upper abdomen. It occurs commonly after meals when spicy foods are consumed or when a person either lies down too soon after eating and/or when the feet are elevated higher than the stomach. The burning begins when gastric juices from the stomach back up into the esophagus, which cannot tolerate the high acid content. The lining of the stomach and esophagus are made of different substances. The stomach can handle the acid that is required to break down the food for digestion; whereas, the esophagus merely serves as a passage canal leading to the stomach. Similar irritation can be caused from an ulcer or gastritis. Perhaps you have seen television ads promoting a variety of

CHAPTER ONE: HOLY HEARTBURN

products to relieve the burning pain just described. Advertisers for certain medications never seem to suggest changing one's diet. Society tells us to live life to the fullest no matter what harm is caused by our actions. There seems to be a remedy available to mask any adverse condition brought about by our life style.

The setting for the dialogue that Luke recorded between Jesus and the two disciples was on the road leading to Emmaus. Two men were walking from Jerusalem discussing the events that had transpired the past week: the arrest, trial, and the execution or crucifixion of Jesus of Nazareth, not to mention the burial and disappearance of his body.

As Jesus approached the men from an intersecting road he began a conversation by asking, "Who are you talking about? What is the cause of your concern?" The two men were amazed at the questions that Jesus presented. "Where have you been?" was their first response. "Are you a stranger to the area? Have you not heard what happened in Jerusalem this past week?"

Cleopas and his traveling companion rehearsed with the stranger what had occurred during Passover Week.

CHAPTER ONE: HOLY HEARTBURN

Many of the Jews that had met Jesus thought of him as that Prophet or the Promised One that Moses mentioned. We had hoped he could have been the One, but the priests and Jewish rulers delivered him unto the Romans to be crucified. Before leaving Jerusalem, we heard that certain women had visited the gravesite. While at the grave, the women claimed to have had a vision of angels. The angels told the women that Jesus was not in the tomb. To prove their testimony the angles showed them the empty space where the Nazarene had been laid. Two of the Apostles went to the tomb to verify the women's claim that the body was indeed missing. At this point Jesus began to challenge their lack of knowledge of scripture and reminded them what Jesus had been teaching the past three years. Then he [Jesus] said unto them (v. 25), *O fools, and slow of heart to believe all that the prophets have spoken.* (The two men still did not recognize the bold stranger as Jesus.) Jesus was upset due to their ignorance; therefore, he began to teach the two men prophetic truth about himself. He began with Moses in verse 27, *And beginning at Moses and all the prophets, he expounded unto them in all the scriptures the things concerning himself.* Has anyone wondered what Jesus could have taught? Possibly he could have chosen from each book in the Old Testament a picture of himself. Since He was the

Chapter One: Holy Heartburn

word, He could have easily quoted any text, or He could have mentioned each Old Testament book, one-by-one, there by giving a picture of himself.

For example:

Genesis –	He was the Creator
Exodus –	He was the Deliverer
Leviticus –	He was the Sin Offering / Scapegoat
Numbers –	He was the Star out of Jacob
Deuteronomy –	He was the Cities of Refuge
Joshua –	He was the Angel standing in the Way
Judges –	He was the Righteous Judge
Ruth –	He was the Kinsmen Redeemer
1 & 2 Samuel –	He was the Shepherd King
1 & 2 Kings –	He was the Glorious King
1 & 2 Chronicles –	He was the Priestly King
Ezra –	He was the One to restore the Temple
Nehemiah –	He was the One to restore the Nation
Ester –	He was the Protector of Israel
Job –	He was the Mediator
Psalms –	He was the Rose of Sharon
Proverbs –	He was the Instructor
Ecclesiastes –	He was the Chief Good
The Song of Solomon –	He was the Finest of 10,000

CHAPTER ONE: HOLY HEARTBURN

Isaiah –	He was the Messiah
Jeremiah –	He was the Weeping Prophet
Lamentations –	He was the Man of Sorrows
Ezekiel –	He was the Restorer of God's Glory
Daniel –	He was the Great Rock
Hosea –	He was the Healer of the Backslider
Joel –	He was the Hope of Israel
Amos –	He was the Husbandman
Obadiah –	He was the Savior
Jonah –	He was the Resurrected One
Micah –	He was the Witness
Nahum –	He was the Avenger
Habakkuk –	He was the Holy One
Zephaniah –	He was the Judge
Haggai –	He was the Desired of All Nations
Zechariah –	He was the Righteous Branch
Malachi –	He was the Healer of Righteousness

When the men came to a fork in the road, Jesus pretended to walk ahead while the two men turned toward Emmaus. The disciples encouraged the stranger to continue with them because the hour was late and it appeared he was not carrying any food for his journey. Jesus went with the men and continued his teaching about himself through

Chapter One: Holy Heartburn

supper. During the dinner, Jesus took some bread, blessed and broke it and gave it to his two companions. Upon eating the blessed bread, their spiritual eyes were opened and immediately they recognized Jesus as, the Prophet himself. Once they learned who was talking to them, Jesus vanished from before their eyes. The men must have sensed something different about their traveler, because they testified one to another, "Did not our heart burn within us while he talked with us along the way and while he open to us the scripture?" (Luke 24:32)

Does your heart burn with excitement when you hear the truth preached from God's word? Does your heart burn when you read the Bible? Have you read the Bible through from Genius to Revelation? Each time a person reads Scripture, he learns more about God. My wife and I had a friend who read the Bible through five times a year. After his passing his wife told us that they, as a couple, had read the Bible through an additional 164 times during their marriage. If I became stumped over a portion of scripture as to its location or spiritual meaning, I would call Scott for the answer. He truly will be missed.

When was the last time your heart became full, burning with love for the Savior as you read the word? Have

CHAPTER ONE: HOLY HEARTBURN

you ever experienced a burning compassion to share the word of God with someone? What does the Bible mean to you? Can you go a day, three days, or a week without seriously reading the scripture? Or are you still confined to the "Daily Bread" Christianity or some other devotional? Have you read the New Testament through this year? When was the last time you turned to the Old Testament? If someone wanted to know how to be certain of heaven when he died, could you show him from the Bible, or would you have to call your pastor or deacon?

If you have never experienced a ***Spiritual Heartburn***, there are three possible reasons. First, you may not be saved, which means you do not have the oil of the Holy Spirit in which to burn. "He that has not the Spirit is none of His." Second, you may have slipped into a carnal state void of anything godly. Third, you may have allowed the flesh, the world, and the devil to misdirect your attention or defeat you from the start.

Let Us Discuss How One Might Develop a Holy Heartburn
Christ must be first in your life!
The first illustration on how Christ should be first comes from Paul Lee Tan's, *Encyclopedia of 7,700 Illustrations*, (1979).

Leonardo De Vinci was commissioned to paint a

CHAPTER ONE: HOLY HEARTBURN

fresco of the Last Supper. During the three years he took to complete the mural, he tried a number of mediums. He settled on the tried and tested water pigment that was commonly used for frescos. He arranged the Apostles into four sets with Christ in the middle holding a chelas in one hand. An artist friend went to visit the master artist and was taken by the detail and realism of the painting. His attention was drawn to the cup in the hand of Jesus. "The cup seems to jump off the wall," his friend said. Immediately Leonardo took a brush and dulled the luster of the cup saying, "There should not be anything that would detract from the figure of Christ." (#653)*

Someone said that Christ is not valued at all unless He is valued above all, even if it is a mere drinking vessel.

Luke reminds us of what Jesus said, "If any men come to me, and hate not his father, and mother, and wife, and children, and brethren, and sisters...he can not be my

*From Encyclopedia of 7,000 Illustrations, Paul Lee Tan.
Reprinted by permission of Bible Communications, Inc.

disciple." (Luke 14:26) The text does not cancel out other verses that clearly state that we should love the members of our family and neighbors, but rather is picturing that our love toward Jesus should outshine the love for family that it would appear as hate. We need to be careful not to substitute religion for Christ Himself. "And He (Jesus) replied to him, You shall love the Lord your God with all your heart and with all your soul and with all your mind (intellect). This is the first great (most important principal) and first commandment" (Matthew 22:37-38, Amplified, 1987). Ministers need to be watchful not to place their work of the ministry in place of developing an intimate relationship with Christ. The work of the ministry implies building larger barns (churches) and letting the needs of the people fall by the wayside. Therefore, is Christ the center of your life or is your job? Are you replacing serving Christ with building large citadels called churches (for pastors) or more expensive homes for average Christians? Is your primary focus on making money or making time to walk with Christ? I am afraid the general Christian has misplaced Christ by moving him back on the shelf of life. Jesus asked Peter three times if he truly loved him. Remember, Peter found the empty tomb but still took seven of the Apostles fishing the following day. Peter was replacing following Christ with the cares of this life. Jesus, reminding His chief

CHAPTER ONE: HOLY HEARTBURN

Apostle of what is more important, instructed Peter to "strengthen the brothers when he was fully converted." In other words Jesus was saying don't misplace preaching the good news with fishing.

If you walk with Christ on a daily basis, when the fiery furnaces come, Jesus will be with you. Daniel prayed three times a day; therefore, when he was thrown into the lion's den, he merely continued to pray as before. It was not new to him, nor did he need to get into practice. An angel was dispatched to keep him company through the night and the lions at bay. Friends, do not expect to be delivered when you ignore Christ day-after-day and week-after-week. To ignore the word for one *week* will make one *weak*! Peter must have taken the words of Jesus to heart because the Apostle exhibited boldness, *Now when they saw the boldness of Peter and John, and perceived that they were unlearned and ignorant men, they marveled; and they took knowledge of them, that they had been with Jesus* (Acts 4:13). Can people tell that you have been walking with Jesus?

One evening Dr. Charles Weigle, composer of the hymn, *No One Cares For Me Like Jesus,* was presenting the music in a revival service in Pasadena, California. During a free

SLEEPING SAINTS 11

CHAPTER ONE: HOLY HEARTBURN

time the composer visited the famous rose gardens before the evening service. Later that evening, Dr. Weigle was setting on the front pew waiting to sing. A man seated behind him leaned over and asked him how he liked the rose gardens. "Yes, I quite enjoyed them," he quickly replied. He then turned and asked the gentleman how he knew he had visited the gardens? The gentleman said, "The aroma of the roses is still on your clothing" (Paul Lee Tan, #7142).*

In the same way people can tell if you have a daily walking partner. *Thou lovest righteousness, and hatest wickedness: therefore God, thy God, hath anointed thee with the oil of gladness above thy fellows. All thy garments [smell] of myrrh, and aloes, [and] cassia, out of the ivory palaces, whereby they have made thee glad,* (Psalms 45:7-8). A spiritual aroma will transcend upon anyone willing for a close relationship with Jesus. My prayer is that I may walk so close to the Lord that the fragrance of His grace might permeate my being – that my face might glow as bright as the face of Moses when he came down from Mount

*From Encyclopedia of 7,000 Illustrations, Paul Lee Tan.
Reprinted by permission of Bible Communications, Inc.

CHAPTER ONE: HOLY HEARTBURN

Sinai. David said, "My heart was hot within me, while I was musing the fire burned: [then] spoke I with my tongue" (Psalms 39:3).

A true man of God will prepare his thoughts, attitude, and renew his relationship with Christ by spending time with the Savior before speaking to any congregation. Likewise, believers should confess any sin, correct a wrong attitude, and renew a friendly relationship to a fellow Christian (if at all possible) before he makes himself part of any congregation. To make any kind of impact on society, we need a fire upon our hearts, when our spiritual fires catch flam, we can freely speak of the love and grace of God and witness people being saved on a daily basis (Acts 2:47).
The question remains: "How does one develop a Holy Heartburn?"

The Best Way to Walk With Jesus is to Walk Through His Word

In the scriptures we can find:
A life that can never be understood
A righteousness that can never be tarnished
A peace that can never be diminished

Chapter One: Holy Heartburn

A hope that can never be disputed
A glory that can never be clouded
A light that can never be darkened
A strength that can never be made feeble
A beauty that can never be marred
A wisdom that can never be baffled
A purity that can never be defiled
None of heaven's resources can be exhausted

(Author unknown)

We should remember that the two men that were on the road to Emmaus could not keep to themselves the news that Christ was indeed alive. Luke 24:33-35 tells us, *And they rose up the same hour, and returned to Jerusalem, and found the eleven gathered together, and them that were with them, [s]aying, The Lord is risen indeed, and hath appeared to Simon. And they told what things* [were done] *in the way, and how he was known of them in breaking of bread.* Their hearts burned with gladness. They left their supper in the middle of the night and returned to Jerusalem. I remember that Jeremiah could not remain quite even in discouragement; he had to speak (Jeremiah 20:9). When the lepers that

CHAPTER ONE: HOLY HEARTBURN

discovered the enemy had fled (2 Kings 7:5-9), they too returned to the city with the good news. They returned to a community where they were outcasts. Paul also had to preach, "Woe is me if I don't share the good news."

Is your heart burning with excitement today? Are you excited about learning more about God? Are you thinking about a person right now that needs to hear that Jesus died for them personally? Is Jesus real in your life? Does your heart burn with grace and love when you sing the old hymns? Why not leave this service [or when you finish reading this chapter] with the same burning heart and desire the two men had as they returned to Jerusalem to share the same truth that Jesus lives. **Jesus lives!**

Do you have the assurance that your name is written and sealed in the Lamb's Book of Life? If you have not asked Jesus Christ to forgive you of your s-i-n, (singular) that causes you to commit sins (plural), you may doubt your own salvation. If there is the least bit of doubt, you need to make sure of your salvation before you pillow your head tonight. Christian, do you love the **world** more than the **word**? Is there more love for the business than the church? Has your spiritual fire died so low that there is only a hint of smoke? Ask the Holy Spirit to blow on the embers of your heart as

Chapter One: Holy Heartburn

you lay the proper kilning of faith and works in place. God will cause you to burn again. With a Holy/Spiritual Heartburn, there is no need for an antacid. In fact, we need to cultivate heartburn for the saddened; for the sick and dying; for the depressed; for the lonely in heart, and especially for the lost. Do you have a Holy Heartburn?

Notes:

Paul Lee Tan, *Encyclopedia of 7,000 Illustrations*. Rockville, MD: Assurance Publishers, (1979), Illustration # 653.

Ibid., Illustration # 7142.

— CHAPTER TWO —

LEAVING THE SAVIOR BEHIND

Text: Luke 2:41-50

The Setting:

Joseph, Mary, and Jesus had journeyed to Jerusalem, as it was customary among all Jews to observe the Passover followed by seven days of unleavened bread. The first Passover was held in Egypt in the days of Moses. The time/day was called Passover because God provided a way for the "death angel" to pass over certain homes and properties. The death of the first born was the final plague to hit Egypt.

To escape the death angel that God sent against Egypt, a person had only to apply the blood of a lamb to the door post and to the lintel of his home as Moses had instructed. Exodus 12:22 says, *And ye shall take a bunch of hyssop, and dip [it] in the blood that [is] in the [basin], and strike the lintel and the two side posts with the blood that [is] in the [basin]; and none of you shall go out at the door of his house until the morning.* The blood pictures, of course, the crucifixion of Jesus when his hands were nailed to the cross and the crown of thrones pierced his temple. John Foote used Exodus 12:23, "...the Lord will pass over the door,..." for the premise for his hymn, *When I See The Blood.* Sadly many hymns like this one that mentions the blood have been taken from scores of church hymnals. From what I have recently observed, not many of today's pastors are preaching messages about the soul saving blood. I believe we need to get back to the "Book" and its true message ***that Jesus saves!*** If we did, I am sure we would see a change in our churches, families, and even our nation as a whole.

The memorial of Passover is the reason Joseph, Mary, and Jesus had traveled from Nazareth to Jerusalem. The purpose of the concourse is that on the return trip Jesus was left behind. The couple went a day's journey before discovering that Jesus was not among any of the other travelers. Perhaps Jesus' parents thought He would be with friends or would find His way back to them.

Chapter Two: Leaving The Savior Behind

Have you been left behind? It is different from being "home alone." Being left means that you were some place other that home and the people who were with you deserted you. While managing an Exxon station, I met several families traveling together in order to share expenses like Joseph and Mary must have done. Children were left behind because they had wonder off and the parents did not realize they were missing until later. Of course, when a large group travels together, confusion is to be expected. Most caravans always had someone appointed to count noses before the cars left the station. Once, a wife was left behind at my service station. After a visit to the restroom, she stepped next door to the 7-11 Store during which time the three station wagons continued their trip to Miami on the way to the Keys. The lady panicked before she became angry. I suppose the laughter of our personnel did not bring comfort to the situation. I assured her she will be rescued. About thirty minutes later one of the wagons returned to the station. A smiling and somewhat embarrassed gentleman got out of the car and asked if anyone had seen a lady that appeared to be lost. I stepped out from the office where the abandon and sulking wife was sitting to play my part in the soap opera. I asked, while trying to keep a straight face, what the missing person looked like and what was she wearing? I further inquired how he discovered that his wife was missing. He said that about half-way to the toll plaza he noticed that the car was quieter than usual; therefore, he took another nose count and found that his wife was indeed missing from the group. I stepped backward two paces and motioned to the gentleman by pointing in the direction of wife and asked him, if this young lady was the one he had misplaced? An angry embarrassment filled the air. I tried to defuse the situation before World War III erupted by reminding them that people have been left behind before. I said, considering the number of people from three automobiles roaming around in a small area could cause confusion. Besides, now they had something to tell the people back home, and the children had a good story to write in English class about their summer vacation. I bought sodas for the family and reiterated that it was an easy thing to do under the circumstances. Both spouses had smiles on their faces as they pulled out to resume their quest.

My I ask a few questions this morning: Have you left Jesus behind in your life? Have you even realized the fact that He is missing? Have you begun searching for Him? May I further inquire; do you want Him back in your life? Do you want Him part of the family and in the church? Let

CHAPTER TWO: LEAVING THE SAVIOR BEHIND

us examine the original text found in Luke 2.

Jesus Was Left Behind in Jerusalem. (v. 43, 44)

The oversight of leaving Jesus behind in Jerusalem was because Joseph and Mary were busy with the details of the return trip.

Many people get wrapped up in the cares of this life and leave Jesus standing by the wayside. We have developed a society that moves at a fast pace. We have to rise early; we hurry to the school, to the job, and to the store. Many people are found running here and there but never taking time to enjoy living in America. To describe our helter-skelter life style, we have coined the phase "rat race" because mice seem to scamper around the maze without getting anywhere. We refuse to use the time that God has given all of us to enjoy the benefits of a good job that allows us to purchase the upscale homes in good neighborhoods. American families are seldom home but rather are out running here and there working extra hours hoping to earn enough to pay their bills. I love the commercial on television that shows a man with everything: a new house, car, a membership in a country club, and nice clothes. In the last scene he tells the television viewers that

Chapter Two: Leaving The Savior Behind

he is in debt up to his eyeballs, and adds, "Please help me." People like the man in the commercial are so busy keeping up with the Joneses that they are leaving Jesus behind – totally out of their lives. Society is in a hurry. We do not want to wait on anything or anyone. We speed down the highway cutting in and out of traffic in order to get to the exit or the next street first. We rush through the checkout hoping to get out of the door before the person in the other isle.

Our vacations are so rushed that we need time to unwind from the vacations. We have fast foods, fast car washes, fast oil changes and laundries; we can have a pair of glasses made in an hour, and by all means, we need the latest computer because it responds quicker than the one bought last year. On the other hand, everything is going about normal: work, bills, taking kids to sports practice, a few sick days, car repairs, etc. But have you forgotten to take Jesus with you? There are those who believe man is placed on planet earth to fin for himself. Others believe that we should not bother God until a crisis arises or until a catastrophe strikes. The truth is that Jesus would like to be with you to witness your good days, such as the promotion at work or the home run at the game or even the five pounds you lost on your diet. Nevertheless, we tend not to find time to pray

CHAPTER TWO: LEAVING THE SAVIOR BEHIND

or read the Bible until a family member has to go to the ER, lays on his or her deathbed, ends up in jail, or files for bankruptcy. Friends, Jesus wants to be part of the good times as well as the bad. It might come to the point that you fail to talk to God long enough, that when something does occur, God may ask, "What did you say your name was?"

We should remember that God is a transcendent Being – He involves Himself in His creation. Everyday He went to visit Adam in the Garden in the evening. They would walk together and talk about Adam's daily activities. God wishes for fellowship. I believe that hardships often come to stop man's fast-pace life style to get his attention in order that he might ask for assistance.

A wise Chinese father gave his son a living inheritance on monthly installments. Six months past when the son asked his father the reason he set up such a program, "It would be easier for me to have my inheritance in one lump sum," said the son.

"I know," replied the father, "but that way I would never see you enjoy the benefits of my hard labor nor would I see my grandchildren grow up." The Chinese parent

Chapter Two: Leaving The Savior Behind

enjoyed the visit from his son and family regardless how brief it was. When was the last time you thanked God for what you have – a good job, good health, a well and loving family, etc. Like the Chinese father, God the Father wants fellowship or an intimate relationship with you, His Child.

God remembers you. He keeps the gravity working, the oxygen in the air, your hearts beating, the sun burning, and the earth rotating; He keeps the soul saved and the devil at bay. The Church at Ephesus (Revelation. 2:4) did not **lose** their first love, they **left** their first love! (My emphasis.) There is a difference between loosing something by accident and leaving something behind on purpose. The Christian zeal died or at least had cooled down in the church at Ephesus at the time of John's vision – the cause is unimportant. We must realize that it is difficult to remain motivated 24/7. The world makes more noise as the days go by and along with her lights and greater temptations, directs our attention away from Christ and His Church. A Christian can leave Jesus behind. A carnal Christian leaves Jesus behind on purpose like the Prodigal Son. The temptation of the world and of the devil is strong adversaries to overcome. Besides, we tend to rely on our money, education, and people we know to help us through life. Churches are

CHAPTER TWO: LEAVING THE SAVIOR BEHIND

relying on the charisma of the pastor, advertisement, or the professional music programs to entice visitors to the service. Others rely on the sign out front or the denominational ties to bring people to their church. They seem unwilling to call upon the Holy Spirit for assistance. They may not have heard, there is a Holy Spirit.

There Could Be Non-Spiritual Causes For Leaving Jesus Behind

Society and some churches have drifted so far away from God that they do not realize that Jesus is missing. In the popular book series *Left Behind* by Tim LaHaye and Jerry Jenkins (1995), man is left behind due to his lost condition following the rapture of the church, not God. The true Christian goes home to heaven to escape the period known as the Tribulation. The Tribulation is the seven years when the earth is purged of sin before Jesus can set up His millennium Kingdom. Some faiths teach a carnal Christian that has left God out of his daily life so much so, he will not be included in the rapture of the church. [This is not a true biblical doctrine.] Paul said in 1 Thessalonians 5:9, "For God hath not appointed us [the Christian or Church] to wrath,..." Those who will be left behind may believe that people disappeared

CHAPTER TWO: LEAVING THE SAVIOR BEHIND

as a result of weather conditions, earthquakes, or even UFOs, since God promised to send strong delusions to all those who did not believe.

Joseph and Mary left Jerusalem following the Passover. *And when they had fulfilled the days, as they returned, the child Jesus tarried behind in Jerusalem; and Joseph and his mother knew not [of it]. But they, supposing him to have been in the company, went a day's journey; and they sought him among [their] kinsfolk and acquaintance* (Luke 2:43-44).

It took a full twenty-four hours to make the discovery that Jesus was nowhere to be found. Joseph and Mary began their search among friends and family. If a friend or neighbor came to you searching for Jesus, could you direct his attention to the proper scripture in the Bible to answer their questions or would you have to call the pastor?

Verse 45, tells the reader that the parents could not find their son. Please note that the couple did not tarry where Jesus was not present. They did not stay to fellowship; their quest was urgent. How much time do you spend with people who are not Christians – who are not walking with

Jesus or do not attend church? Do you spend more time with the secular world than with the saved? Do you spend more time in the world or in church? We should remember [not to], *Love the world, neither the things [that are] in the world. If any man love the world, the love of the Father is not in him. For all that [is] in the world, the lust of the flesh, and the lust of the eyes, and the pride of life, is not of the Father, but is of the world.* I John 2:15,16 and James 4:4 reminds us not to be friends with the world since such friendship is enmity with God.

Joseph and Mary Returned to Jerusalem (v. 45).

The parents had a day to catch up. One day's travel from Jerusalem had to be retraced. Two days without their son; what could have happened? What were Joseph and Mary thinking for these two days? (What would be going through your mind if your child was missing?) They may have asked themselves, "What did they do wrong? Could this have been prevented? Maybe he fell in with the wrong crowd or among thieves." The parents retraced their steps from entering the city a week before. Possibly as they searched, they were thinking of the good times, fun times, or the quite times they had had. They were trying to fill their

Chapter Two: Leaving The Savior Behind

minds with positive thoughts as their search continued.

When was the last time you and Jesus went for a quiet walk: through His word; through the fields of nature – observing the flowers, clouds, animals – thanking and praising Him for all creations, or through the tough streets or neighborhoods of service extending a hand to the needy; assisting people who do not know the Savior on a personal level. When people see you, do they see Jesus? We need to be with others as we are with Jesus. We say we love Jesus, but do we really love Him? Have you ever noticed two people in love? They walk hand-in-hand. They appear to be in their own private world. Everywhere you see one, you see the other. Circumstances do not bother them, they are in love. The rainstorm does not faze the couple – they are in love. When they are separated, they are always talking on the phone, just because they are in love. We say we love Jesus but allow a child's sniffles to keep the whole family home from church. We allow clouds of the day or a few snowflakes to keep us from church but never from the golf course. We add excuses of being tired when we had a hard week at work, or that we have to wash the dishes or service the car. We can come up with 1,001 excuses to stay home Sunday morning. Where would we be if Jesus decided not to come to earth; if He made excuses not to be baptized?

CHAPTER TWO: LEAVING THE SAVIOR BEHIND

Where would we be if Jesus decided not to visit the garden of prayer? Where would we be if Jesus decided to side-step the cross; "I am tired and I do not cherish being whipped and nails driven in my hands and feet and a crown of thorns pressed on my brow." Does Jesus live with you or is He knocking on your heart's door to come in?

It Took Another Day To Locate Jesus

Do not expect to live a life of woe for a long period of time and hope to feel great relief at your first prayer of repentance. Forgiveness is instance, but fellowship has to be renewed. For example, the wayward son had to first return home, wash, and change clothes before going to the banquet. How long were you out in the cold world? How long did it take to develop the calluses on the soul so that you no longer feel pain? The same calluses prevent you from feeling love. If a distant runner brakes training just a couple of days, he will have to practice almost an entire month to get back to the level he was in his training. The same thing applies to being a carnal Christian. One prayer of repentance and one church service will not place a person on shouting ground. Such a person will have to get used to the church environment again, singing hymns, and discipline his life for renewing his acquaintance with God. By reading the Bible and

Chapter Two: Leaving The Savior Behind

developing a consistent prayer life would be the first steps one needs to renew his relationship with Christ. The renewal will not be accomplished overnight or even in a few short weeks. It will take time.

Joseph and Mary may have searched the room where they stayed for the past week. Anxiety could have been mounting as parents retraced their steps through the city. Consequently, the Jesus you are searching for cannot be found in religion or by keeping the Ten Commandments. Furthermore, a person cannot find Christ in the social clubs, country clubs of nobles, at bridge games, sports arenas, or on the lake fishing. Where did the parents find Jesus?

The Parents Found Jesus In The Temple (v. 46)

Possibly the Temple was the last place the family was before leaving the city. There is a better chance to find Jesus where other Christians gather – where the word of God is preached and true prayer is rendered – where faith is exercised and miracles are seen.

Jesus' parents were amazed, and *when they saw him, they were amazed: and his mother said unto him, Son, why hast thou thus dealt with us? Behold thy father and I have sought thee sorrowing,* (v. 48). Jesus appears to have been in the Temple for three days, talking and asking questions of the priests and religious leaders. I never tire of true questions about the Bible. I rejoice in answering questions of hungry minds and tough questions keep me sharp and dependent on the Spirit.

The parents questioned Jesus with the statement, "We have been searching in sorrow." Who sees sorrow today or even humility in the church by those who are searching for Jesus? How many people do you see coming for salvation with tears and sorrow? How many people do you see rejoicing once they have salvation? I am afraid a number of today's redemptions are merely head knowledge – not heart acceptance. If my observation is correct, most of the people that come have never found Jesus, only a satisfying copy or counterfeit to fit their lifestyle. Others have adopted spiritualism, cults, education, works, church membership, or church broads as a substitute for God's salvation.

They have rejected the simple salvation by grace through faith and not through good works because most people want to have a working part in their redemption. The average man wants to be able to say that he found Jesus himself; that

Chapter Two: Leaving The Savior Behind

he came to God on his own terms, not on God's terms.

Dear Christian, have you left Jesus behind? Do you have a noticeable emptiness, heartache, or loneliness? Have you noticed the little but consistent problems in life? Are you actively seeking to locate Jesus? Are you searching in the right places?

An ax head fell in the river in 2 Kings 6:5, 6. The prophet was willing to help relocate the ax head, but he needed to know in what area the man lost his instrument. In the same way you must retrace your tracts of your life to determine what influenced your life to deter you from the narrow way leading or following Jesus. If you make a wrong turn off the interstate, you must go back to that exit in order to make the proper correction that will allow you to resume in the right direction.

For those who are not Christians; those whose life is in total chaos; you only need to call to Christ. He will find you where you are. You may have acknowledged Jesus as savior, but in your heart you know there has not been any change – no joy or assurance. You doubt your name is written in the Lamb's Book of Life. Salvation is free; Jesus will make Himself known – only call upon Him today!

CHAPTER TWO: LEAVING THE SAVIOR BEHIND

Notes:

John W. Peterson, ed., *Great Hymns of the Faith*. Singspiration Music, Grand Rapids, Mich: (Zondervan Corp.), Song, "When I see the Blood," #232.

Tim LaHaye & Jerry B. Jenkins, *Left Behind*, (vol 1). Wheaton, Ill.: Tyndale House Publishers, Inc.

Chapter Two: Leaving The Savior Behind

— CHAPTER THREE —

Parable Of The Sower, Seeds And Soils

Text: Matthew 13:1-10

Introduction

A parable is a form of communication or a means of telling a story that conveys certain implied truth. Familiar or common items are used in the narrative to link the known realm to the unknown or spiritual world. Jesus used the people's knowledge of planting and harvesting a garden to convey the needed spiritual truth of receiving the word of God and the reality of having the spiritual seed mature enough to produce fruit.

Chapter Three: Parable Of The Sower, Seeds And Soils

The Apostles had a problem grasping the true intent of the parable; therefore, they asked Jesus to interpret His teaching in order to understand its meaning more fully. A spiritual application is revealed from Jesus' response (vs.11-17) as well as the means to show the further truth hidden in other parables. The historical context should be considered in any interpretation: to whom was the parable given and who was its author? For example, each gospel writer, guided by the Holy Spirit, had a certain audience in mind and a certain point he wished to stress. Mark's writing was presented as an epic because Jesus rose from a difficult beginning to the ultra victor found in the resurrection which the Romans liked and accepted. Luke wrote to the Gentiles in general, whereas John seemed to be writing to everyone. Matthew focused on the Jewish population because of his Jewish heritage. Each gospel writer presented Jesus in a different genre with a different audience. Mark viewed Jesus as a servant who worked His way up through society to become the Savior of the world. Luke's medical background allowed him to show Jesus as the son of man; thus, his gallery became the average person on the street. John took the other direction by proving Jesus was the Son of God. Matthew traced the genealogy of Jesus through the Jewish spectrum and presented Him as the King of the Jews through King David.

CHAPTER THREE: PARABLE OF THE SOWER, SEEDS AND SOILS

Let us direct our attention to the parable in question. It mentions a sower, seed, and four different types of soils or gardens where the seed was sown. The fields represent the hearts of individuals or the intellectual capacity to receive spiritual truth. For example, Nicodemus (John 3) did not understand the statement, "You must be born again." He did not fathom that man must have a spiritual rebirth to be able to stand before a Holy God. Because the Holy Spirit plays such an important part in the spiritual rebirth, Jesus used the wind as a metaphor for the Holy Spirit. But Nicodemus questioned, "How can all this be possible?" To which Jesus responded with a question, "Are you the teacher of Israel, and yet do you not know nor understand these things?" Jesus continued trying to explain spiritual truth to this teacher, "If I have told you of things that happen here on earth, and you refuse to believe, how you can believe, if I tell you heavenly things?" (Amplified) Paul had the same problem accepting revealed truth on the road to Damascus. After Jesus spoke to the Paul, the persecutor, the would be Apostle must have wondered about what was presently occurring because Jesus knew that Paul was kicking [rejecting] against the goads, (Acts 9:5). I chose the word "reject" because what Paul was hearing went against all

Jewish tradition and teaching of his priestly training.

The setting for the parable of "the sower, seed, and soils," was not in the temple because the Jewish leaders did not accept Jesus as a true prophet, not to mention, the Messiah. Therefore, Jesus went to the common people who were more likely to believe the Messiah had come as did the woman at Jacob's well. A small boat served as a pulpit and the water of the lake was used to amplify His voice so all those that were gathered could hear. The message began with a person going out to sow seed in four different gardens or four different types of soils. The disciples asked Jesus to interpret the parable (v. 19-23). The original sower of seed was Jesus (John. 1:1) and the seed was the word of God. The four different grounds represent four types of people and how each would receive the seed of the gospel. The only thing that has changed in 2,000 years is the person doing the sowing. The modern day sower is the evangelical believer. God's word is still the seed and the variety of people remains the same. The following four points explains how the individual hearer responds to the word of God and why. I will attempt to show possible reasons certain Christians and non-Christians have problems understanding spiritual truths. I further hope to reveal a way to overcome many of life's difficulties.

CHAPTER THREE: PARABLE OF THE SOWER, SEEDS AND SOILS

Some Seed Fell on the Wayside (v.4)

We must examine the term "wayside" first. A wayside seems to imply it is the side of a road, if the "way" represents a route of travel. Therefore, the wayside is not literally considered a chosen place in which to plant seed. What was Jesus implying when He scattered seed on such a non-respective ground? He wanted everyone to have an equal chance to respond to the gospel, not only an elect few. He made "everlasting life" available to all. No one will be able to stand before the loving and just God and say he was not given an opportunity to accept forgiveness. I have no problem with sowing seed on the wayside. The characteristics of this ground accurately describe a certain type of person that seems to make up a larger section of society every year.

Because there is no loose earth to cover the seed, there can be no germination of the seed. The question must be asked, "What caused this person to be so packed down or his conscience so hardened that there was no feeling, knowledge, or desire left to cover/accept the seed?" This individual possibly had been kicked around by the world so long that he had developed calluses, an area upon the heart that no longer had the sensory ability to feel. Maybe he had been turned off by the inconsistent philosophies he had learned in college. He may have grown hardened from the lies people are apt to tell over and over. The hypocrisy experienced in the world and seen in the church can easily cause a heart to harden over time thus, preventing the person from rightly receiving the truth of the good news. This would prevent any response from or to Jesus. For example, He could not work in His hometown of Nazareth because of unbelief (Matthew. 13:58). Throngs of people refused to believe the words of Christ when He tried to prove who He was by performing miracles. Masses of people seemed more interested in receiving free fish and bread or witnessing a miracle than understanding spiritual truth that would set them free from the chains of sin.

Scripture teaches us that not everyone will believe. Continual unbelief will make it difficult for people to be saved. If unbelief progresses to the stage of the reprobate (Romans 1:28), it seems by definition that such a one will no longer be savable. It appears God will withdraw the Spirit of conviction thus, allowing the rebellious sinner to live out his life but void of any urging of the Holy Spirit to repent unto salvation. Many Christians do not like to view God in this manner. They like to see God portrayed as a

CHAPTER THREE: PARABLE OF THE SOWER, SEEDS AND SOILS

loving father who always would be willing to forgive. He will forgive, but only through His Son, Jesus Christ. God is longsuffering and not willing that any should perish. Critics of a judgmental God often forget that God is Holy. His character and attributes must allow Him to deal with sin. When judgment becomes necessary, there will be a time when God will say, "Enough is enough," as in the days of Noah (Genesis 6) or when Israel entered into the 70 years of captivity (Isaiah 39: 6-8; Amos 7:11). The Everlasting Father over the years has been urging the lost person to repent during the first two stages that are found in Romans, chapter one. God gave His people up first to uncleanness, and secondly to vile affections before giving them over to continue in their reprobate thinking. This shows God is longsuffering. He does not rejoice over the death of a single sinner. Those critical of this doctrine of rejection, must realize that we do not know how many years the Father has been trying to bring the lost into the fold of His Kingdom. Be assured, God never forces His love or grace upon any person. He gave man a free will to accept or to reject Him. The Sadducees rejected Peter's teaching of the resurrection. Members of the Sanhedrin would not receive Stephen's testimony even though, "they were cut to the heart," or fell under conviction through guilt of what they had done to

CHAPTER THREE: PARABLE OF THE SOWER, SEEDS AND SOILS

Jesus. Their compassion was so far removed that the religious crowd was seen literally biting the deacon (Acts 7:54) for his witness before they stoned him to death. How many people believed the words of Noah, Moses, or Jeremiah? (Lest we forget, the work of the Spirit is to soften the heart or plow the soil of the believer; thus, enabling him to receive the seed of truth. God is the only One who sees the true intent of the heart.)

The first ground of the Mathew 13 parable typifies a person where the seed remained on the hardened surface. This type of person could be considered closed-minded or those who would not get anything from a sermon or personal testimony. One could say such a person is "dead from the neck up;" they have a heart of stone – past feeling, etc. The mind and heart will not accept metaphysical love or truth. They have no desire for change. They do not recognize that God may exist and may have denied personal sin, as well as the existence of an after life. Their condition does not exempt the believer from sharing the truth of God. Such rejection should cause our hearts to weep.

The seeds do not remain lying on the surface of the ground. The text states that birds came and stole the seed

CHAPTER THREE: PARABLE OF THE SOWER, SEEDS AND SOILS

before the soil could change its consistency. Jesus labels the birds as workers of Satan. Unless a clean bird is named specifically, birds in general are considered unclean and evil. In the Book of Daniel, King Nebuchadnezzar's vision of a large tree was depicted as his kingdom. The fowls perched in the tree pictures the possible presence of evil lurking among the good for an opportunity to disrupt. Satan is seen in the Book of Job walking up and down the earth in search for someone to tempt. The wicked city of Babylon, prior to her fall, (Revelation 18:2), will be "the habitation of devils and home to every foul spirit, caged, and unclean and hateful bird."

If the demons steal from the lost, I believe they are as prone to do the same to the Christian. For example, what was the pastor's message about last week or the week before? How much difficulty do you have remembering scripture? Christians should have enough loose soil to hide the seed until it is heated by the Holy Spirit and watered by God's grace to allow germination to take place for the plant in order to grow and produce fruit.

I remember having a garden when I was growing up in North Carolina. A scarecrow would be constructed and

CHAPTER THREE: PARABLE OF THE SOWER, SEEDS AND SOILS

placed in the middle of the garden to frighten away the birds. Mother would also run a cord over a newly seeded row from which aluminum pans were hung. Between the sun's reflection on the pans and the noise they made from hitting one another was hopefully enough to frighten the birds away.

The analogy of the scarecrow and flashing pans can be seen as answers to the prayers of the person who sowed the seed. Angels, representative of scarecrows, may be sent to keep the devils from stealing the word before it had time to germinate. I believe we who sow seeds for the present generation have the responsibility of keeping the birds/devils away from new seed or tender plants as Abraham kept the birds away from his sacrifice (Genesis 15:11).

"What causes the spiritual hardening of the ground?" must be asked again. My idea is that it comes from one's attitude. Has the reader ever had sharp words with family members Saturday night or Sunday morning before church? If so, he is packing the soil down making it difficult to receive seed from the pastor's message. An argument after church allows the birds to steal whatever spiritual seed may have been thrown in one's direction. A prideful, selfish, or unforgiving

CHAPTER THREE: PARABLE OF THE SOWER, SEEDS AND SOILS

attitude will cause the heart to be unable to receive any spiritual instruction that came from the morning message. The devils on both accounts know where man is most vulnerable; thus, they can set the stage for a family argument that would quench the receptive power of the Holy Spirit.

Some Seed Fell Upon Stony Places (v. 5)
The garden full of stone or rocks represents a heart full of worldly cares and a life of deadly lusts. There is loose soil but it has no depth. Rocks lay upon the surface as well as beneath the soil. The seed would sprout into small plants, but because the loose soil was shallow, the small roots would not have the strength to penetrate the rocks or enough substance needed to go around the barriers in search for good soil. The water supply would be too deep and the rocks too large for the tiny plants to drop their small roots to the needed level.

Every spring after the garden was plowed, my family would walk the plowed earth and pick up or dig out large rocks before it was raked and leveled for sowing. We were unsure from where the new rocks came from since this process was practiced every year. Seemingly the rocks just reappeared. The rocks in the parable symbolize the different

Chapter Three: Parable Of The Sower, Seeds And Soils

cares or sin that has entered a person's life and in so doing prevented spiritual maturity and growth. A person must determine what rocks need to be removed but ***he must do the excavation himself.***

In my opinion one of the major problems among Christians is that they want someone else to remove their rocks. A number of Christian counselors and pastors seem to have a naïve understanding how spiritual obstacles are removed or how problems are solved. The many pastors and most church members appear to expect God to work miracle after miracle solving problems that arise after a brief time of prayer. Generally, after the pastor listens to a person tell about his problem, he shares a few scripture texts to be read through the week by the counselee. When their time together ended, both parties promised to pray for God to intercede in solving the problem. The problem seldom disappears after such a brief time of counseling. Please do not label me an unbeliever. I believe in prayer and I believe the Bible carries the answers man needs for his life's walk, but the Christian needs to be responsible for his own actions. More of an explanation will be given later in the essay.

A person unfamiliar with how God actually works

Chapter Three: Parable Of The Sower, Seeds And Soils

may question, "Where is the supernatural working of God? I have prayed for such and such; where is the answer?" I believe the supernatural work has been done when the Holy Spirit gave man the faith to believe in Jesus Christ (Ephesians 2:8, 9). He has prepared the believer's heart to receive the gospel seed. God supplied the preacher or neighbor to deliver the seed in a message or personal witness. The Bible said that the Holy Spirit will supply another person to give the water of encouragement, or a further witness. "I have planted, Apollo watered; but God gave the increase," (1 Corinthians 3:6).

When God made the earth and everything in it, He gave each living thing the power to grow and reproduce. From the earth green grass grows; a cow eats the grass that goes to produce milk, which in turn man drinks. The supernatural is seen in the grass, the cow, and the milk. Notice, man must put forth some effort to milk the cow before he can drink. What am I saying? I am merely pointing out that God has provided the necessary ingredients for the human race to produce spiritual fruit, but it takes labor on man's part to continue the process that leads to maturity. Before the fall, Adam and Eve lived in a perfect environment where everything was supernaturally made available. After sin entered the equation the residents of the Garden were expelled; thus, Adam and Eve had to work in their own strength in order to eat and find shelter. Likewise, physical labor is required today in order to have a spiritual garden. The supernatural work is still seen in the *earthen vessels* that gives the spiritual seed power to grow. Since man came from the earth (Genesis 2:7), he must depend on the earth for life, *And God said, Let the earth bring forth the living creature after his kind, cattle, and creeping thing, and beast of the earth after his kind: and it was so. And God made the beast of the earth after his kind and cattle after their kind and every thing that creep[s] upon the earth after his kind: and God saw that [it was] good* (Gen. 1:24, 25). The writer of Genesis continues this thought in verses 28-30: *And God blessed them, and God said unto them, Be fruitful, and multiply, and replenish the earth, and subdue it: and have dominion over the fish of the sea, and over the fowl of the air, and over every living thing that move[s] upon the earth. And God said, Behold, I have given you every herb bearing seed, which [is] upon the face of all the earth, and every tree, in the which [is] the fruit of a tree yielding seed; to you it shall be for meat. And to every beast of the earth, and to every fowl of the air and to everything that creep[s] upon the earth, wherein [there is] life, [I have given] every green herb for meat: and it was so.*

Chapter Three: Parable Of The Sower, Seeds And Soils

The third chapter of Genesis reveals how sin entered the perfect environment with the temptation of Eve and the fall of Man. Sin and the persons responsible for sin must be judged. God began with the serpent from which the allurement to disobey God came. All serpents, after this time, were sentenced to craw on their stomachs. They were never allowed again to walk upright. Next, the Holy Creator informed Eve that she and all women after her would suffer pain during the birth of a child. God's final judgment fell, not upon Adam directly, but upon the ground from which Adam was formed. From this time forward, man will have to labor by the sweat of his brow in order to eat. The earth, because of the curse laid on it, would not be friendly toward man. It would produce briars and weeds to remind man of his sin.

The New Testament clearly states that without works one's faith will be in vain. Prayer is the faith part and works is the physical part. For example God told Joshua that He had given the new land to Israel, but Joshua and his people learned they would not have a "cakewalk." Claiming the land was one thing, homesteading it would be something else. The entire nation had to fight for it and win the battles before the promise was fulfilled. It is not always enough to simply encourage an individual to pray and for the counselor to promise to pray for them. This could give the person the wrong idea that problems will be supernaturally removed without the personal involvement. When the difficulty remains, the believer is instructed to pray more or harder (whatever that means). Sometimes people are told to merely "hang in there" until God intervenes. Miracles are not an every day occurrence or they would not be considered miracles. It seems a number of church leaders do not consider that there could be causes for an individual's perplexity or that the person may need help in devising a plan or some other needed assistance to obtain victory. The person may be spiritually deaf or he may not be used to listening for or hearing the Spirit's counsel as young Samuel learned in 1 Samuel 3:1-10.

The rocks do not only typify sin, although many will, some rocks will fall under the category of mental and emotional disorders. In those situations the individual may need help with deciphering his or her real problem. He may need certain tools or strategies on how to dig up and/or brake up larger rocks. Some can be easily cleared away while others will require more time and labor. The best encouragement I have received came from a Christian

Chapter Three: Parable Of The Sower, Seeds And Soils

counselor, who later became my mentor in the counseling field. He advised me not to give up on more difficult problems, but to begin chipping them into manageable pieces that could be more easily handled and removed. If this policy is practiced, an immense anomaly can be soon cleared from one's life.

• • •

Please allow me to share one of many personal experiences. A friend phoned me out of her fear of secular psychology to ask for help concerning her daughter, who was washing her hands almost 50 times, a day. Her condition is known as obsessive-compulsive disorder or OCD. A promise was made to research the matter. I found no pastor or Christian counselor among 127 local churches able and/or willing to help. It seemed they did not work with individuals with "mental or clinical emotional" problems. One church counselor stated that his church only ministered in marriage and family difficulties. I thought to myself, if a person carries the title **Christian Counselor,** he/she should avail himself or herself to learn something about mental and personality disorders in addition to scriptural knowledge like my Christian mentor had encouraged me to do. If not, the church is inviting the troubled person to seek assistance elsewhere who may not have a Christian philosophy.

• • •

There are two schools of thought listed under Christian counseling: The first school is **Nouthetic Counseling** where the only text book seems to be the Bible. This view sees man as a dichotomy, a creation equating the soul and spirit as one. Only three sources are viewed lending to personal problems under this school of thought: personal sin, demonic activity, or organic illness. It denies any form of non-organic mental illness better known as psychological problems.

The second school carries a similar title of **Christian Counseling**. A more accurate label could be *Christian Psycho-Therapy*. This school of thought uses both Scripture

CHAPTER THREE: PARABLE OF THE SOWER, SEEDS AND SOILS

and the science of the brain and mind to promote healing. Generally, "Christian Therapy" does not accept *everything* from the different secular schools of psychology, but at the same time, agree that man is made up of the emotion, will, and spirit, which incorporate the mystical part of man. This includes accepting the conscious and unconscious working of the mind. For example the brain can be seen but not the mind, but we know the mind exists nonetheless.

Because of certain secular beliefs among psychologists and psychiatrics, such as evolution, animalization of man, and the denial of the existence of a Supreme Being, most Christians in general and pastors in particular have shied away from considering any validity psychology has to offer. Likewise, psychology has denied the metaphysical or spiritual side of humanity. Thank God both sides are presently taking a fresh look of these neglected areas. Because the church has almost divorced itself from the needs of life in the world, the ministry is unable to properly sheppard the individual soul. For more than one reason scores of people remain either lost and/or neglected in the shadow of the cross. It would amaze both schools of psychology of the amount of research that has been done in this subject and recorded in the vast number of scientific

Chapter Three: Parable Of The Sower, Seeds And Soils

journals in the past thirty years.

Meanwhile, since a local Christian counselor was unable to be located who was trained in compulsive disorders, a competent counselor from out of town recommended a trusted family physician be called. The doctor was called and understood the mother's concern and the daughter's disorder. A simple medication for depression was prescribed which eliminated 60 to 70 percent of her hand washing. Proper Christian counseling could now ask the right questions to determine the cause of her disorder. Symptoms of OCD are not listed in scripture, but the general causes leading up to the disorder could be.

• • •

While on the subject of where Christians should seek assistance, I would like to share another personal experience of having rocks in my own garden. I once suffered anxiety attacks for about three months. Several times a day or night it felt like a shroud of fear dropped over me. I met with a pastoral counselor who practiced *Nouthetic counseling* in a local church. His primary solution to my problem was prayer, but little else. Because I was a minister and hopefully knowledgeable, in his eyes of scripture, he merely reminded

CHAPTER THREE: PARABLE OF THE SOWER, SEEDS AND SOILS

me of familiar scriptural texts I should read while I described my problem. He had the belief that true Christians should not suffer as I was describing; thus, he was unwilling to seriously accept my condition as psychological or look for a root cause. He surmised my problem could be a spiritual attack. (A number of evangelical pastors believe the fallen angels, turned demons, wage daily attacks on Christians. The Bible does list such assaults on God's people. For example, King Saul (1 Samuel 18:10-12) became paranoid and was troubled with great fits of depression; the Apostle Paul (2 Corinthians 1:8) suffered not only untold physical conflict, but was under great stress that he even despaired to continue living.) The Christian counselor hurriedly fished for possible reasons for my unrest. His only suggestion besides reading the Bible and praying was to cleanse my home of all "suspected" demonic material. Most pastors, like me, do not knowingly allow harmful artifacts of Satan to enter the home. Nevertheless, I followed his directions without questioning further or considering the lack of any hard evidence of an evil presence due the current mental state I was experiencing. [I never had experienced such symptoms as these. Matter of fact, the condition I was suffering "blind sided" me. I have never experienced such despondency.] Looking back, I believe there was a slight

CHAPTER THREE: PARABLE OF THE SOWER, SEEDS AND SOILS

coercion to destroy a comic book collection, the only so-called "rock" the counselor found in my garden. Were the comics the catalysts that brought on the anxiety? I believe not, but rather a scene from a television show would be more feasible.

• • •

Mental science is unsure what triggers sudden anxiety or panic disorders. The best therapy to combat this disorder seems to be psychoanalysis, where the counselee is coached to talk about the present fear that is causing the problem. The Christian community should not be afraid of psychological language. **Psychotherapy** is merely talking things out with the hope the root cause will be revealed. **Cognitive Therapy** is where reasoning comes to the aid of the individual. Through questioning and answering a diagnosis as to the cause can be determined. **Behavior Therapy** considers what action or behavior the person is currently doing or has done in the past. Scripture teaches, "Change of thought brings

CHAPTER THREE: PARABLE OF THE SOWER, SEEDS AND SOILS

change of behavior." Solomon said (paraphrasing), "As a man thinks in his heart, so is he" (Proverbs 23:7) In other words, a person's actions can be influenced by his thought life.

• • •

After a month with little relief, I began to question the diagnosis and the prescription of merely praying and *rebuking* the devil. This brought me to the point that I had to begin my own research (from my personal library on anxiety and phobias) and approach prayer in a different manner. I prayed for the Holy Spirit to guide my endeavors to find relief and cure. I realized that I had to take responsibility for my own healing. I knew the answer had to be in the word of God, but I had to take an active part; therefore, all imaginations of fear that were filling my mind had to be cast down. All thoughts had to be held captive, (2 Corinthians 10:5).

One division of man's soul is his will. I can will myself to think negatively or positively. In the beginning it was not easy to redirect my thoughts to be more positive, but I knew it was possible. With discipline and reason, I continued

CHAPTER THREE: PARABLE OF THE SOWER, SEEDS AND SOILS

casting away the undesired thoughts that flooded my mind. In a short time the attacks of anxiety subsided. But the average Christian sitting in the pew would not have the same resources or training as I have had to begin the healing process. The only hope left for such a person would be to go a trained Christian counselor, psychologist or psychiatrist.

I did seek advice from a former church member during my self-help search, who was a licensed psychologist and Christian and soon to be my counseling mentor. He made some suggestions. "Do not panic!" was his first advice. Panic brings thoughts that all is lost with no hope. Such rash reasoning will bring further frustration and possible thoughts of running away from the event or even suicide, what he called "the coward's way out." It is amazing how fast the mind, especially with the help of evil spirits, can flood the brain with such abstractions. His second suggestion for me was "Do not to make snap decisions without first considering all avenues." He further explained that most disorders that develop reveal only the tip of a larger problem. Scientists are still unsure how phobias develop (out of the blue) without warning. In our discussions neither Warren, my spiritual counselor, nor I ruled out a spiritual attack. Secular counselors seldom, if ever, admit a

Chapter Three: Parable Of The Sower, Seeds And Soils

problem could be metaphysical in nature. James wrote, Resist the devil or his evil thoughts and he will leave you alone (4:7, Paraphrased).

In my case, I believed there could have been a spirit of fear, imagined or otherwise, that came upon me. Cognitively, I reasoned the chance of dying ruthlessly was absurd. The anxiety attacks revealed the general frailty of my flesh. Theologically, it proved that Satan wanted to destroy the witness of Jesus Christ. Psychologically, I encouraged myself with the belief that there were supernatural powers standing ready to defend God's name and God's disciple. For example Jude writes a powerful promise in verse 24, "Now unto him that is able to keep you from falling...." Paul writes, "Being confident of this very thing that he which [has] begun a good work in you will perform it until the Day of Jesus Christ," (Philippians 1:6, NKJV). I often use the following promise of 1 Timothy 1:7 in my counseling sessions which reads [paraphrasing]: "unjust and paralyzing fears do not come from God; rather He bathes His children in power and love, and gives them a sound mind or right thinking." What gave me the victory was turning off the television for a period of time (not wanting any diverse stimulus), discarding the rocks of doubt and fear, coupled with a steady diet of reading God's word (the correct stimulus), continuing prayer (focusing upon my soul within), and renewing the "armor of God" which is spiritual in nature, Ephesians 6. Because of what I learned from my experience, I believe that I will be able to help others who suffer the same or similar afflictions as I did. (1 Corinthians 1:4).

Some may believe that Christians should never have doubts, anxiety, or any other problem, but Paul serves as example of a *strong* Christian who did: "…we were pressed out of measure, above strength, insomuch, that we despaired even of life" (2 Corinthians 1:8b). This sounds like someone in desperation or at wits end with a desire to die to find peace. Since Paul endured and won the victory, what should the present day Christian do with the modern advantages and knowledge available to him?

Trained Christian counselors are available in most communities. Biblical commentaries flood the market along with a vast number of texts on psychology. Science has made great progress on how the brain and mind function. Doctors have been able to pinpoint areas of the brain by using x-rays and MRIs that are responsible for certain emotional conditions. Research continues making great

CHAPTER THREE: PARABLE OF THE SOWER, SEEDS AND SOILS

inroads in this area. The Christian counselor and/or pastor should avail himself or herself of this research.

I think of all the work that our forefathers had to perform before a single biscuit could be eaten. The land had to be cleared, plowed, and raked before the seeds were sown. Afterwards, the wheat had to be harvested, ground into flour and properly mixed, and then baked. The point I'm trying to make is that God gave us His word for examples to follow. He used practical illustrations common to His day in order for men and women to understand what He was saying. *If physical labor is required to maintain physical life, spiritual labor must be necessary to maintain a spiritual life.* [There is a bridge linking the two realms of life.] The Bible is filled with illustrations to encourage the believer to remain faithful in both areas. Yes, God answers prayer, but He also requires His children to do certain things for themselves.

The Lord's teaching of removing stones from a vineyard (Isaiah 5:1-2) pictures God's preparation for Israel to become a great nation. After plowing and preparing a place for the chosen people, a fence was constructed around the land to protect the tender nation from any invading force

CHAPTER THREE: PARABLE OF THE SOWER, SEEDS AND SOILS

seeking to harm God's people. The next step applies to the current Matthew 13 parable of gathering stones (v. 2) from the field. This would remove any obstruction that would hinder the growing process. It would mean the removal of other nations or philosophies. The tower that was built speaks of God's watchful care that coincides with the next ground where the enemy sowed tares among the good plants.

A practical prayer for strength should be the next step in removing the rocks from one's spiritual/physical life. The two natures of man affect one another. Scores of books are currently on the market depicting a relationship between the mind and body. The mind is representative of the soul/spirit. Discouragement comes when one only prays for the rocks to somehow miraculously disappear only to wake up in the morning with the same rocks or urges still in place. Many can testify to how difficult it is to stop smoking or drinking alcohol or giving up pornography or gambling, etc. Others may have a problem with lying, gossiping, overeating or low self-esteem or even fear. Some rocks will be more difficult than others to remove. They can come in a variety of sizes and weights; in addition, they can lie instead at different depths in the soil.

Chapter Three: Parable Of The Sower, Seeds And Soils

After 30 years in the ministry, I have found that the tendency for a number of people is to pray around the blockage or hindrances they are experiencing. They will pretend, during the counseling session, the burden is not a big problem, when actually the bolder is twice or three times as large under the ground as it appears on top of the ground. When difficulty continues, the person must realize he must begin removing smaller rocks or he may give up on ever overcoming sin or seeing disorders healed in his life. Removing small rocks in the beginning builds confidence enough to tackle the larger ones.

There was a man in a former church that never could clear his life of personal barriers. His paranoia and bipolar psychosis would defeat him before he got started. Early on in my ministry, I had to learn that some good people would sabotage their own prayer and labor in order to remain in the same condition. Life to them would be like playing a ball game from the dugout or locker room. Being expelled from the game becomes their comfort zone or their way to escape personal responsibility. They are actually afraid of the reality of entering the game. If they play, they would have to be responsible for how they handled themselves on the field. Taking responsibility is risky and uncomfortable for

CHAPTER THREE: PARABLE OF THE SOWER, SEEDS AND SOILS

some; therefore, the trend would be to remain on the bench or in the locker room of fear. Between games the person would emerge to complain of his handicap to others with the hope that he would receive pity. General caregivers must realize there will be those who will never obtain victory. On the other hand, with the proper teaching and a little labor, great numbers could ascend to a higher level with a little more spiritual discipline.

A few poor souls, who try to play the game of life, believe that victory can be won by having others play the game in their place or by regularly changing teams completely. For example I have had church members make the rounds through the membership of other churches or to the point of joining another church in order to request assistance and prayer. Each visit the person made gave opportunity for him to express all his problems and difficulty he was having. He would often show up just in time for a free lunch. The person was hoping to use the prayer of others as a magic wand or *Thor's Hammer* to break-up his rocks that seemed to be causing him problems. He was hoping the other person could do the job for him, but he would always have some rocks hidden that he would treat as a personal possession. To be sure God has a hammer

CHAPTER THREE: PARABLE OF THE SOWER, SEEDS AND SOILS

(Jeremiah 23:29), i.e., His Word, which overrules any tool Greek mythology can construct.

Rocks come with different names

As I stated before, there are surface rocks and others that lay out of sight to the average onlooker. I will not dare name every possible kind of rock – each field is unique. The individual will have to determine what kind of rocks he has in his own garden. The following serves only as a primary guide for excavation. There is no precise order nor can I say that one's obstacles are on the surface or buried. Hidden rocks do tend to be one's secret sin or the main cause of psychological disorders. Rocks most prominent will be resentment, anger or hate followed by fear, worry and anxiety. These are common in most gardens. Others to look for could be unbelief or lack of faith, self-centeredness, unresolved guilt, inferiority attitudes, and uncontrolled desires (different types of lust) to name a few.

Man's three natural enemies according to scripture are the flesh, the world, and the devil. Paul and James realized what problems the flesh could cause (Romans 7:17-20; James 1:14-15). Disciplining the flesh means keeping it under the control of the will. This is a lifelong task. Paul urged everyone to die to self or to the flesh on a daily basis. John wrote in his first letter not to love the world: *Love not the world, neither the things [that are] in the world. If any man love the world, the love of the Father is not in him. For all that [is] in the world, the lust of the flesh, and the lust of the eyes, and the pride of life, is not of the Father, but is of the world. And the world passeth away, and the lust thereof: but he that doeth the will of God abideth forever* (1 John 2:15-17). We often forget that the world has a curse on it from Genesis 3. If God destroyed the world with water (2 Peter 2:5) the first time, what kind of fiery judgment is down the road for the next up and coming generation? (2 Peter 3:7).

Satan is the author of sin. By deception he tempted Eve to sin and, in turn, caused Adam's fall. The Devil introduced sin to the human race through Adam (Romans 5:12); the temptations of the world adds fuel to the situation. By this time man's fallen nature kicks in and he tumbles into trouble with open eyes.

Most often a weakened or deceived individual believes it is impossible and/or too painful to remove the rocks from his field. It may take time, but it is most important to begin the process with prayer. Prayer is the

CHAPTER THREE: PARABLE OF THE SOWER, SEEDS AND SOILS

power source for the Christian to contend for the faith. The person with all the proper armor in place will tire quickly without prayer (Ephesians 6:18) When Aaron and Hur lifted the hands of Moses (Exodus 17:10-12) toward heaven, it pictured the importance of prayer for those in the valley who were engaged in battle. Before victory was won, Moses grew weary and let his arms fall to his side. When the arms were lowered, Joshua began to lose the battle he was fighting, but upon raising the prophet's arms, Joshua began to regain lost ground. This narrative also shows the importance of having friends while you wage your spiritual battle. Moses is the man of God; Aaron and Hur serve as his prayer warriors while Joshua was leading the battle with the help of his army. Therefore, picture yourself in the valley battling against different kinds of barriers or rocks in your life. A person needs someone to hold his name up before God as he labors in removing his rocks. He may need others to assist in his work (not actually removing your hindrances, but giving water of encouragement and by calling on God's angels to strengthen you as you continue working). A trusted friend could hold the person in question accountable for his labor without becoming judgmental.

CHAPTER THREE: PARABLE OF THE SOWER, SEEDS AND SOILS

Do what you can on a daily basis

One could begin the process of removing smaller rocks and work up to the larger ones. Conquering smaller sins builds confidence and shows the task is possible to perform. To make a large rock movable, he may have to chip or break it into manageable pieces. Each small piece that is discarded represents *yardage gained,* or less of a hindrance in one's life. This will lead to a first down and eventually scoring a goal. Enough touchdowns will lead to victory. To keep track of one's progress, he/she could mark a calendar in red for all the small victories and use black for temporary setbacks. When I became tired of all the black marks that filled my calendar, I earnestly prayed for strength to do what must be done. God answered by directing my attention away from the flesh, the world and failure. Focusing on positives gave me strength and the willingness to remove more rocks that prevented any maturity from occurring.

Second, rocks remain in a person's life because he does not have anyone to stand with him or to suggest that victory can come in small steps rather than in one leap. A young child will be unable to enter a weight lifting competition because of his size. Neither could I enter a 100-meter race without first spending time training for the event.

CHAPTER THREE: PARABLE OF THE SOWER, SEEDS AND SOILS

Coaches play an important part in an athlete's training. When I said a person might need assistance, I did not mean that the helper would remove any rocks from the person's spiritual garden. Another person can not run the race for him, but his friend could hold him accountable. Sometimes a person may need to ask for accountability assistance. The helping coach would keep in contact through the week and offer encouragement and may suggest better ways of attacking his spiritual field.

Pastors, caregivers, or counselors (after making a correct diagnosis of the cause for the problem) should be knowledgeable enough about discounting certain hindrances to list certain steps the believer could do to begin clearing his spiritual landscape. The client should be encouraged to call with a weekly report of work that has been completed or if he has at any time stumbled or became discouraged. A former member used to phone me when he felt like going on the Internet to view pornography or even when his thought process entered that area. To assist him further in breaking up this extra large rock, his wife took the modem of the computer that allowed access to the Internet while she was at work. For many this particular rock will be hidden deep in the shadows of the soul. (More about hidden rocks will be revealed below.) Removing any size rock or sin will free up a vast portion of the person's spirit to allow good seed to be sown. Checking on one's progress is the same philosophy the Alcoholics Anonymous employs. It is also referred to as the "buddy system."

Hidden rocks are the most difficult to remove

Hidden rocks that lay below the surface can not be seen by the general public and may even go unnoticed by the individual landowner. The person may not know the reason he or she is going through certain difficulties. The spiritual surface of the soul seems clear of all rocks of sin. At this juncture, it is important for the person to be consistent in church attendance and personal Bible reading and prayer because the Holy Spirit knows where the hidden rocks are and is willing to reveal and assist in their removal. A person can have a medical problem but the cause is not evident. The doctor will call for x-rays and blood test to be performed. Christian counselors often perform the same type of tests as the one listed above but for the soul. Without accepting the shedding of blood on Calvary, there can be no remission of sin. Does the person know for sure that he or she is saved? The Christian counselor must determine if the person having

CHAPTER THREE: PARABLE OF THE SOWER, SEEDS AND SOILS

problems is truly born again. If not, the use of the Bible as a spiritual medicine bag or even prayer will have a limited affect on the person in question. Jesus gave us a blood transfusion when He shed His blood on the cross: His righteous (sin-free) blood replaced our sin-polluted blood. (Romans 5:12, 8; Hebrews 9:22) Another test may require an x-ray; the Holy Spirit (through the preaching of the Gospel or from reading God's word and through prayer) may direct the individual to look in a certain area of his spirit for hidden cancerous rocks that could be poisoning the soul. Failure to do so could result in a physical illness erupting.

People with rocky gardens can be their own worst enemy; thus, they can circumvent the evacuation of the very item that is causing problems. He may have put forth little effort, but decided that he had done all he could. He may view the garden full of rocks and tell himself there are too many and give up trying. Or possibly he has a sin or disorder that he enjoys – [I call this the "pet rock syndrome."] This is one's private or hidden sin; the one he believes is not harming anyone or the one he most enjoys regardless of the consequence. Those are the sins and rocks that become decorative or enjoyable. A person who smokes may say he enjoys it; a person who is hooked on drugs may believe he is not harming

CHAPTER THREE: PARABLE OF THE SOWER, SEEDS AND SOILS

anyone else but himself. If that is okay, this person does not see that he is a slave to the drugs. The drugs prevent good health. Rocks in the garden prevent the plants from growing and producing fruit. The devil is consistently whispering negatives in the person's ear as he did Eve's. If the surface of the garden is clean, but there remain certain areas where grass or flowers fail to grow, the owner may have to excavate the needy areas. Professional counselors may have to be called in to probe the area. Once the cause of the deadness is determined, the owner must make the decision to tackle the problem head on. Hidden barriers must be dug up and discarded in order to have an abundant life.

The sun becomes an adversary (v. 6)

The first garden had birds come and steal the seed from the wayside. In this garden the reader sees the sun serving as a persistent adversary apart from the rocks. Perhaps this is when the devil enters the picture. The tender plants would have difficulty growing roots over, around or through the rocks. In addition the plants could not find the needed nutrients or water to sustain them; thus, the plant would become scorched from the sun and die.

The interpretation that Jesus gave is found in verse

CHAPTER THREE: PARABLE OF THE SOWER, SEEDS AND SOILS

21. He equated the sun to tribulation and/or persecution. Satan can institute tribulation (problems) whereas, persecution, under the direction of the devil, comes from man. Believers need to learn that life will be filled with problems. A Christian carries the nature or gene of sin even though he is saved. Furthermore, he is walking on a planet that has been cursed. The devil never tires and never sleeps. Because of the power of the Holy Spirit, the devil is unable to prevent a person from becoming saved, if that person chooses to be saved. God made man a free moral agent. (Forced love is not true love.) God never demands that man love Him in return (Romans 5:18), but the Devil may suggest to man, due to his problems, that God does not love him. At the same time, the devil may cause enough problems to bring defeat and loss to any Christian if the believer allows him to do so. Peter was walking on the water as long as he was unconcerned with the storm. It was when Peter's attention was redirected away from Jesus (to worldly affairs) that he began to sink. He was redeemed only when he called upon Jesus to rescue him.

Jesus forewarned the disciples there would be days of turmoil. He warned them against being deceived; warned them that there would be wars, famines, pestilences, and earthquakes (Matthew 24:4-7). These could be classified as typical troublesome times common to all. Verses 9-11 speaks of persecution, *Then shall they deliver you up to be **afflicted**, and shall kill you: and ye shall be hated of all nations for my name's sake. And then shall many be **offended**, and shall betray one another, and shall hate one another. And many false prophets shall rise, and shall **deceive** many.* (emphasis added). The reason for all the problems is found in the last four words of verse 9, "for my name sake." This coincides with the text (Matthew 13:21)**:** "…because of the word by and by he is offended." In other words the sun represents natural problems that will occur and because of the believer's identification with Christ and his preaching or testimony, persecution will follow.

Paul admonishes Timothy in 2 Timothy 1:8 not to be ashamed of the testimony of the Lord. As there were those like Jannes and Jambres who resisted the truth in the days of Moses, (2 Timothy 3:8) there will be those who in this age will resist the same truth. Presently, there seems to be an attack being waged upon Christians in general. American courts are ruling against displaying the Ten Commandments publicly and forbidding public prayer in many areas. Children at school or adults at work cannot display the Bible, wear

CHAPTER THREE: PARABLE OF THE SOWER, SEEDS AND SOILS

crosses, or even bow their heads silently in prayer. The ACLU's newest attack is upon city seals that display a Christian emblem such as a cross or Bible. Surprisingly, nothing is mentioned about emblems of other faiths. The attack seems to be directed mainly against the Christian faith.

As the day of Christ's return draws closer, the sun of persecution will become hotter to the point that it may evolve into a super nova as in the days of Rome when thousands of crosses filled with crucified Christians lined all roads leading into the city. The Christian community must get its garden ready by removing as many rocks as possible; thereby, allowing him or her to drop his roots (in faith) in God's spiritual aqueduct. This, in turn, will permit the plant (Christian) to mature and produce fruit as God had intended for the harvest prior to the famine. *Behold, the days come, saith the Lord GOD, that I will send a famine in the land, not a famine of bread, nor a thirst for water, but of hearing the words of the LORD: And they shall wander from sea to sea, and from the north even to the east, they shall run to and fro to seek the word of the LORD, and shall not find [it]* (Amos 8:11-12). I detect the beginning of a famine of God's word presently. In some countries, including America, pastors are forbidden to mention portions of Scripture because the courts

CHAPTER THREE: PARABLE OF THE SOWER, SEEDS AND SOILS

have ruled that they are now considered "hate speech." Secondly, the gospel has been watered down (through the many of the modern versions of scripture) as to not offend anyone under the sanctions of the deacon board or church councils. There is documented evidence that Holy Scripture is being erased from the public square. The print media continues criticizing the Bible and the people who believe it by sowing doubt toward its founder and formation. This describes the rocky ground.

Some Seeds Fell Among Thorns (v. 7)

The first seeds fell upon hard ground where the soil was packed down; thus, the seed remained on the surface available for birds to steal. The second handful of seeds fell upon a rocky terrain. There was enough loose soil to partially cover the seed. This allowed a small plant to form but because of the surface rocks and those under ground, the tender plant was blocked from finding enough water to help it bear up under the hot sun. The third handful of seeds fell on seemingly better soil than the two prior gardens. Small plants sprung up and began to grow. All seemed well for the new plants, but there was an enemy hiding in the soil. It is known as the human nature of mankind. The adversary came from the original curse of Adam. The serpent was sentenced to crawl

CHAPTER THREE: PARABLE OF THE SOWER, SEEDS AND SOILS

on the ground; the woman (Eve) was cursed to endure great pain during childbirth. Instead of cursing Adam in like fashion, (which would make the human race "unsavable"), God cursed the ground from which Adam came: *"...cursed is the ground for thy sake; in sorrow shalt thou eat of it all the days of thy life; Thorns also and thistles shall it bring forth to thee and thou shalt eat the herbs of the field;* (Gen. 3:17-19). The common name given in the New Testament for thorns is *tares*. I consider any vegetation that will hinder or kill a fruit-bearing plant or tree a tare. This includes vines, grasses, and briars of all sorts. The primary task of a gardener is to keep such weeds from the growing area. I have to pull or cut weeds and grass from the flowerbed that encircles my house every so often. Grass is cut from around many of the fruit trees to enable the roots to breathe.

Spiritual tares can be divided into two classes of worldly tares and mental tares that seem to hinder the believer much like the grass and vines in the yard. Many times the job of weeding the tares becomes difficult because the green weed resembles the good plants in the early stage. For example there is a difference between milk, skim milk, and chalk; yet, they are similar in color. A number of commentaries link the parable that follows the soils with the wheat and tares

CHAPTER THREE: PARABLE OF THE SOWER, SEEDS AND SOILS

(Matthew 13:24-30). The next parable does shed light on interpreting this section of scriptures. Although the second parable reveals that man is not necessarily responsible for all that hinders his walk, there is a different analogy applied to the second narrative (v. 38-43). Because the writer speaks of a harvest in the end times, the wheat is representative of the believer that will be placed in "my barn" or God's heaven. When the tares, on the other hand, are gathered and burned, speak of a lost person being sentenced to hell. The servants are human disciples and are unable to properly discern between the wheat and the tare that is saved or lost. Because man is unable to make the distinction, the reapers (God's angels) are called to perform the proper harvest. They know who belongs to God and who doesn't.

The garden with tares, like the field of rocks, has a spiritual message for every believer. As Christians need to remove the rocks of hindrance before he plants, they further need to pull the weeds from their soul that will, likewise, hinder spiritual maturity. In fact, as the tares work quietly in their camouflage state, they appear like a good plant; thus, making the danger more deadly. The rocks hinder growth whereas the tares *attack* a living plant for the purpose of robbing it of its own nutrients. One can conclude stones

CHAPTER THREE: PARABLE OF THE SOWER, SEEDS AND SOILS

spoil the roots and the vines spoil the fruits.

Problems are said to be part of life; therefore, Genesis 3 shows the reader the troubling tares can be natural. Certain things will come into the Christian's life that wishes to become prominent in that life. It is impossible to prevent the seed from germinating into a plant (the lost being saved), but Satan will use the curse of the earth against the Christian, the Church, and the Kingdom as often as he is permitted. This means that Satan will use man's own sin nature against him. Because the Christian retains his fallen character, regardless of the fact that he or she is a new creature due to the salvation of the soul, it becomes easier for Satan to sow all forms of temptation toward the flesh (James 1:14-15; Romans 7:5).

A second type of tare found in verse 25, can be interpreted as either a life problem or mental problem. I believe it falls more toward man's mental state than physical although it has been discovered that one's mental attitude can and most likely will affect the physical body. I believe part of our battle today is mental because of how the spirit entity places the tare in the life of the believer. *But while men slept, his enemy came and sowed tares among the wheat, and went*

CHAPTER THREE: PARABLE OF THE SOWER, SEEDS AND SOILS

his way. Satan waits until we are at rest to do his dirty deeds. He can misdirect our attention while he sows his evil when we are not looking. Science is presently adopting a new way of determining or locating spiritual or mental problems that has caused physical illnesses. Some call it "Body Works or Body Talk." First developed by those of the New Age Camp, the theory is that the body tries to tell the mind there is a problem and the location of the enigma. I am not advocating a New Age philosophy, but since the body, soul, and spirit of man are interrelated, as seen in scripture, communication between the three seem to be possible. Dr. Gabor Mete's new book, *When the Body Says No* (John Wiley & Sons, Inc., 2003) is a good introduction to consider on the subject. Some practitioners have used the phrase intuition when the answers are not forthcoming. What medical doctor has not used his intuition (training and knowledge) when science has failed to produce an accurate diagnoses.

Has the reader ever wondered where evil thoughts originate? Does an evil thought merely surface from the natural mind of man? Some may, but one should not beat himself up with guilt because he had a bad thought. Everyone has them. It is only when a person continues to meditate on the evil thought that sin begins to grow or produce an evil or sinful

Chapter Three: Parable Of The Sower, Seeds And Soils

act. This could be what Paul was referring to in Romans 7:15-19: *For that which I do I allow not: for what I would, that do I not; but what I hate, that do I. If then I do that which I would not, I consent unto the law that [it is] good. Now then it is no more I that do it, but sin that dwelleth in me. For I know that in me (that is, in my flesh,) dwelleth no good thing: for to will is present with me; but [how] to perform that which is good I find not. For the good that I would I do not: but the evil, which I would not, that I do.* Man seems to retain the nature of sin in his born-again state. The new creature is born when the Holy Spirit enters the spiritual part of man, but does not immediately affect his mental or physical part. James writes that the flesh is where sin resides following a Christian experience because the soul is sealed or protected by the in-dwelling Spirit of God (Ephesians 4:30). If it wasn't, then salvation would only be temporary since sinning anew would result in losing one's salvation. This would not make it eternal as scripture teaches. (1 Peter 1:5; Hebrews 5:9; 2 John 2:25)

The *Amplified New Testament* (Zondervan, 1987) takes a fresh look at the Roman text. If a person does what is contrary to his or her desire, the mind is surrendering to the yearning of the flesh and not of the will. Paul said that it was not he, himself, that was performing the act, but the principle of sin residing in him. The Apostle further said that he had "the intention and urge to do what was right, but had no power to carry it out." Because of this law, the body is still under the sentence of death, "For the wages of sin is death," (Romans 6:23). James concurs by saying when lust is conceived, it gives birth to sin; and sin, when full grown will bring death to the individual. Satan, therefore, uses the natural condition of man when he implants evil desires in the mind of the saved or lost soul.

Matthew reveals how Satan works in the mind of man in the next parable, "But while men slept, his enemy came and sowed tares among the wheat…." Jesus interprets the text in verse 39, "The enemy that sowed the tares is the devil." Two references illustrating this verse quickly come to mind. The first one is found in 1Chronicles 21:1: "And Satan stood up against Israel and [enticed] David to number Israel." There are several sins that David committed in taking a census at this time, but the more important factor is that Satan placed the thought to take a census out of context of God's law, in the mind of the King. The second illustration is found in Acts 5:3, where Peter asked Ananias, "Why hath Satan filled [your] heart to lie to the Holy Spirit?" There are several texts that clearly show how Satan has influenced or

CHAPTER THREE: PARABLE OF THE SOWER, SEEDS AND SOILS

hindered individuals. My pastoral professor warned the class of preacher boys that evil thoughts could come to mind of the best Christian because he has had less than godly thoughts right before the time to preach the gospel. (A quick thought is not sin, but if the thought lingers, it can cause a person to act out the dark idea. Once the thought is put into action is when it becomes sin.) Satan will tempt one to sin, and when the person yields to that temptation, Satan will, in turn, give the individual good case of guilt for yielding to the temptation he just presented. In addition to temptation, Satan attacks the body out right. There were a number of Sundays when I became deathly ill 12 to 24 hours before the Sunday morning service. I found I was not the only pastor who experience a sudden illness prior to preaching. By mid-afternoon the illness left. Satan's purpose seemed to be to stop the gospel from being presented with the possibility of lost souls accepting Jesus as their Savior.

The tare described in Matthew 13:25, is a poisonous rye grass. The Greek word is *darnel* and is referred to as "creeping wheat" or "couch grass" [*triticum repens*]. What makes this unique and dangerous is that it grows underground until it finds a healthy root system. The grass wraps itself around the roots and climbs to the surface to continue its

CHAPTER THREE: PARABLE OF THE SOWER, SEEDS AND SOILS

stranglehold on the plant. The result is death to the plant or the tare will strangle the branches so severely that the branch will be unable to produce fruit.

The tare goes unnoticed in the beginning because its appearance is similar to good wheat. The devil is a master at deception: *for Satan himself is transformed into an angel of light; therefore, it is no great thing if his ministers also be transformed as ministers of righteousness…* (2 Corinthians 11:14-15). Jude writes about what could be considered spiritual tares when he mentioned (v. 4) that certain men have secretly entered the church for the purpose of misdirecting the worship and introducing deadly heresies. Modern man has the technology to make things look like something they are not. Pressed wood is sawdust that is overlaid with veneer. When finished it will look like real wood. Plastics can look like wood or metal. Sadly, modern churches are filled with what I call, "plastic Christians" – all because the "evil one" has planted tares among real believers. Most church splits are the result of tares having been sown among the weak members. Scores of pastors and Christian workers succumb to lustful tares that have crept in unaware until the tentacles are securely wrapped around the victim. Believers start off well and in the right direction but can easily become

CHAPTER THREE: PARABLE OF THE SOWER, SEEDS AND SOILS

distracted by life in general or feel at ease (believing nothing will happen to them) like David. Some faiths teach since a person is born again (child of God), he or she is supernaturally protected from all problems and pain. This is, of course, error of the worst kind, and it will cause a tragic defeat for many. More emphasis is placed on the job rather than the church. Like Peter, the believer can be more overcome by circumstances around him rather than trusting God and His plan. Tares are sown in the church, home, school, or on the job, because the devil can disrupt and bring chaos anywhere he chooses.

The true battlefield is the mind of man. One of the first books written on the subject was Tim LaHaye's book entitled, *The Battle for the Mind*, (Fleming H. Revell Company Publishers). Richard L. Strauss wrote, *Win The Battle For Your Mind*, (Loizeaux Brothers, 1986). The newest book on the subject of mental warfare is by Joyce Meyer, *Battlefield of the Mind*, (Warner Faith, 1995). It is believed that 40% of Americans suffer from some type of mental disorder. Unfortunately, we are responsible for most of the problems that befall us. America is the most restless and discontented nation in the world and, believe it or not, we use more drugs for psychological disorders than any other industrialized nation. It is high time for the church to become more involved with the total healing process for her members. There will always be a need for traditional Bible studies where historical events and personalities are placed in chronological order. Consequently, the majority of ministries overlook another vast mission field of its own members. Evangelism is important, but the saved need to be grounded and pointed in the right direction in order to have a strong church. There is not a Christian church that does not have scores of people sitting in the pews suffering unjustly in some aspect of life. Problems in the family ranks number one: there is someone considering divorce; going through a divorce; or coming out of a divorce. Others may feel alone, neglected, angry, pressed down with guilt; and still others may be experiencing a spiritual attack of evil. If the church is unable to develop classes or studies to meet one or more of these difficulties, it should seek out side assistance from the community or from the denomination. Weak members (plants) will not become strong enough to reproduce themselves. The world will keep rocks of hindrances in their field, and the Devil's demons will continue to sow tares of deception.

Problems, people, and possessions are three tares the

CHAPTER THREE: PARABLE OF THE SOWER, SEEDS AND SOILS

devil uses against man quite successfully. Problems can un-expectantly happen such as a flat tire on the freeway, family illness, or an overdrawn checking account. Problems never happen at an opportune time. God is more concerned with how the believer meets each problem. People, because of different personalities, can be the most trying tare of all. When Paul and Silas were trying to minister God's saving grace to the people in Philippi, a demon possessed girl tried to disrupt Paul's teaching with the spirit of divination. [This essay has only considered spiritual persuasiveness or manipulation. Demon possession needs to be studied separately.] The young girl spoke the truth in this case, when she informed the city that these men were from God (Acts 16:16-18). Her testimony only gave further credence to her employers instead of God because the city knew who she worked for. But like a good gardener, Paul had to pull the weed by ordering the demon spirit out of the young girl. When this occurred, it affected personal finances so much so, that it was relatively easy to influence the entire population to riot. Tares of unrest were sown quickly in the community. The young girl's employers influenced the people and city leaders to have Paul and Silas beaten and imprisoned without a Roman hearing which Paul was entitled to since he was a citizen of the state. The total occurrence seems willfully defeating with the devil winning at every turn, but upon a closer examination of what later transpired, God meant it for good. Down one of the dark corridors after midnight, the jailer and his family came to accept Christ as their Savior by faith and they were baptized. One can be in the will of God even though problems seem overwhelming. Problems should not be considered a place to give up, nor should they be viewed as "dead-ends," but are oftentimes given to be worked through to bring the believer to a higher level of maturity.

Most often people would not consider possessions ever being a tare or – maybe the lack thereof. We understand from scripture the "love" of money is a sin – not the money itself. There is a disorder known as *hording* given to individuals who have an addition of buying "stuff" for the mere sake of having – not that there is any need or purpose behind purchasing the merchandise. When it concerns books, I can fall victim to this tare. It would be different if I had read all of the books my library contained, but I haven't. To overcome this hindrance, I recently promised myself to read at least eight or ten books before buying another one. Keeping this promise has allowed me to catch up on much needed reading. The Bible says that man should be satisfied

CHAPTER THREE: PARABLE OF THE SOWER, SEEDS AND SOILS

with the important things for the day. Being rich is not a sin, but it can become a hindrance to some people. The rich ruler (Luke 12:16-20) planned to build larger storage places to house his wealth instead of giving the excess to a good cause. The question has been asked several times, "How much is enough?" The answer is always the same, "Just a little more." Hours and hours are given over to info-commercials on television that entice the public to believe there is a get-rich-quick scheme. The devil is wise in knowing what personal buttons to push to misdirect one's attention away from the things of God so he or she will not notice being entangled with tares. Lot did not notice the hidden "darnels" (tares), which lay in Sodom; neither did Balaam, Cain, or Korah (Jude 11). What happened to these individuals is found in Jude 12: "…trees whose fruit withereth, without fruit, twice dead, plucked up by the roots."

I believe that Jesus included the illustration of the wheat and tares to show people that they are responsible for pulling up and discarding the weeds themselves. They can ask for prayer (and should pray for themselves) to give them the strength or motivation to weed their soul of everything that prevents proper growth and maturity. The people in question must realize that no one can pull up the weeds for another person. This would be like asking another person to study for a certain test that you must take. Or it would be like asking another person to take a bath in order that you may become clean.

Christian leaders and life coaches who merely suggest clients pray and read the Bible in order to alleviate the soul of the *items* that are causing them difficulty are opening the door to further frustration and depression when the symptoms fail to disappear or when God decrees a miracle is not called for. For example, God can and has healed cancer, but I personally do not believe He will take cancer from a person supernaturally until that person stops smoking or gives up any other activity that could lead to cancer. God will not heal from the effects of a tare when the tare is still attached and growing in the person's soul/body. Prayer becomes more meaningful when the doctor tells the patient all has been done that can be done. This is when miracles tend to happen. One must not forget that Paul had a personal physician by the name of Luke as a traveling companion on many of his journeys. In other words, after a diagnosis is made, the counselor and client should develop and agree upon a plan to eliminate the suspected tares from the damaged soul. The tares may be in the form of negative thoughts or desires. The troubled person most often needs a

CHAPTER THREE: PARABLE OF THE SOWER, SEEDS AND SOILS

specialist to show the difference between the permissive thought and the bad thought. Many Christians need to be made to realize that often times the bad thoughts were not generated by their brain, but were sown from an outside source, the devil. Learning of the true source of one's thoughts lessens the possibility of unfounded guilt that may follow. The devil will temp a person to sin, then criticize him for yielding to temptation. Once the Christian begins the process of beating himself up with irrational thoughts, as the Devil had intended, he can move on to another unsuspecting believer to begin the process again. Let's examine the final garden.

Some Seeds Fell On Good Ground (v.8)

The good ground was prepared to receive seed. It was not packed hard but had been plowed and raked. The good ground was free of excessive rocks that would hinder plants from growing. The good ground, ***in the beginning***, would also be free of all weeds. The owner of the good ground would keep a watchful eye on himself and would not let any form of tare become prevalent among the growing plants of the knowledge of God that had taken root. There will only be a certain number that will grow to maturity and produce fruit. Further interpretation (paraphrasing) of the text is given by Jesus in verse 23: "But he that received seed into the good ground is he that hears the word, and understands it...." This person's heart was prepared to receive the gospel, and the heart was capable of sustaining spiritual truth where improvement and growth was likely.

The reader should not become depressed with the number of needy gardens [3 to 1] in the text in contrast to the single "good soil" that could be in the church. Two of the three gardens could have good soils if and when the rocks and weeds are removed. The scripture teaches for the mature or spiritual believer to help and encourage the weaker brother or sister. Becoming mature enough to bear fruit is not an end in itself. Every Christian is today's new sower and should always have gardens to oversee.

Since the heart of the forth person was well prepared by the Holy Spirit, the person that heard the word ***understood*** it. This individual was not like Nicodemus: "...how can a man be born again when he is old?" (John 3:4). The doctor of law clearly revealed that his garden heart was fallow (packed by law and tradition) in that he asked, "How can these things be?" (v.9). The disciples of Jesus appeared to be slow learners; they each testified that they believed Jesus was

CHAPTER THREE: PARABLE OF THE SOWER, SEEDS AND SOILS

the Christ, but while the men were in a certain town, not a single disciple testified that Christ was just outside the city at Jacob's Well. A young lady, an outcast of the community, talked the men of the city into returning to Jacob's well with her to meet the person who told her all about her life: "Is this not the Christ?" she asked (John 4:29). Because of her single witness the whole community believed (v.42).

Some tomato plants, for example, will be loaded with fruit, while others will only bare two or three tomatoes. Likewise, some Christians will only have few fruit while others will have an average harvest and still others will produce a hundred fold. It is like saying, "The apple tree is loaded this year."

Jesus singled out Peter, James, and John to be his first leaders or chief sowers. Thomas remained part of the eleven after Judas killed himself, but because of doubt he was not separated for greater things [only 30 fold]. Power or faith is given by measure (Romans 12:6); faith was given to everyone as a gift (Ephesians 2:8). It depends on what an individual does with his gift – if he produces 30, 60, or 100 fold. When a garden has been well prepared according to Paul's letter in Galatians 5:22, it can become a major producer of spiritual fruit. We should remember that size does not matter in the spiritual realm. With faith the size of a mustard seed, Jesus said that a person could uproot trees and remove mountains (Matthew 17:20). This encouraged me to believe that my garden could be made good or better, if I began pulling weeds and clearing rocks from my own life. Pastors and church leaders are not exempt from problems or the temptation to sin. Realizing a person has a problem, such as the people who attend AA meetings, is taking the first step in clearing and cleaning his soul of spiritual rocks and tares.

Due to ignorance of how God actually works, my prayers were not being answered as they were requested. During prayer one day, I realized that I had hindrances that stopped spiritual growth and the lack of fruit. The tares and rocks that I discovered did not supernaturally disappear after a simple prayer. I believed prayer guided the Holy Spirit to show me where answers could be found. The "guiding light" led me to the correct scripture to gain insight and motivation to do what was required to rid me of anxiety and to build my self-esteem. He led me to the proper resources that were already in my library that suggested there may be certain tares responsible for my condition. Further research helped me

CHAPTER THREE: PARABLE OF THE SOWER, SEEDS AND SOILS

plan an attack. Strategies were set in place that outlined how to up-root and discard certain hindrances that were causing me discomfort. Time and heartache could have been avoided through proper counseling, but I found none in my area. Anger and disappointment gave way to jubilant joy when I realized that there could be scores of other Christians going through the same experiences as me. This opened a new door for my ministry. I am able to understand what others could be going through and with this knowledge and the love of Christ within, makes me the perfect candidate to become a true physician of the soul.

Those with understanding will bear fruit and, as mentioned above, not every plant will produce the same amount of fruit – some will yield more than others. One should be careful of negative thinking – this hindrance is sowed by the Devil as a tare. He will give low self-esteem to a person who actually has the means to produce 60 or 100 fold, but because of spiritual sabotage will only yield 30 fold or less. A person does not know his true worth or ability until he or she is put to the test. [God allowed certain things to come into my life to strengthen me – not defeat me. He then allowed me to learn that I was not the only person to have these difficulties. Because I learned to overcome, I can teach others to overcome also.] Gideon did not think of himself as a leader for several reasons. He was the youngest son in the family. He was not brave because we first find him hiding behind the winepress. His tribe was Benjamin, the smallest of the twelve tribes. Yet, the Angel of the Lord referred to Gideon at his greeting, "The Lord is with thee, thou mighty man of valor," (Judges 6:12). God proceeded to encourage His future judge with signs and wonders. One can find encouragement through scripture: Abraham, Moses, Joshua, Ezekiel, Peter, James, and John along with other Apostles. The believer, secondly, needs a clear calling or leading from the Spirit, followed by the desire placed in his heart by Him to launch out into the deep. The fruit that is produced could be the first sign a person was walking with God. This small piece of evidence could be all the encouragement one needs to do greater things as he walks with the Lord in this world. We merely present a witness for the Lord: He gives the increase.

If this person representing the forth garden has prepared his heart, the area upon which the seed of the word fell will germinate and grow into a plant. Because of prior preparation of plowing the once fallow ground (with the urging of the Holy Spirit), the removal of excessively large

CHAPTER THREE: PARABLE OF THE SOWER, SEEDS AND SOILS

rocks, and the pulling up of any tare-like vegetation, the stage is set to understand the word in seed form. The softened earth allows the roots of the tender plant to grow toward the water supply. The natural nutrients (innate talents and spiritual gifts) found in the soil/soul, given by God at one's birth and rebirth adds strength to the plant.

Those who do not receive seed properly are explained in verses 14-15. The lost person's heart has grown gross or lays in a fallowed condition. This person does not hear clearly, "their ears are dull of hearing." They may hear the truth, but his soul or mind may not receive it; thus, it will remain as if he heard nothing. A scientist could explain the importance of DNA and how it determines what a person is and the reason he acts the way he does, but because his language (descriptive words) is unfamiliar to me, they dissipate into mere vibrations in the ear. Imagine how long it took people who spoke a certain language to find one another of that language at the Tower of Babel following God's judgment (Genesis 11:6-9). Jesus used the parable as the best form of communication to bring understanding to spiritual matters. Once the seed of the gospel sprouts, the living soul begins a new Christian walk. Eternal life comes only through accepting Jesus as Savior (John 14: 6). Once this happens, the growing and maturing process begins. Fruit bearing is two fold. First, **internal** – "The Fruit of the Spirit is love, joy, peace, longsuffering, gentleness, goodness, faith, meekness, and temperance" (Galatians 5:22-23). These nine traits give strength to the person to produce other fruit. Second, growth is seen **externally** when the Christian reproduces himself. This is when the plant produces fruit or gives birth to another Christian. David said (paraphrasing): He that goes with a sorrowful heart scattering precious seed will in time return rejoicing bringing his harvest with him. (Psalm 126:6) Thus, the parable of the sower and the soils concludes with Jesus' recommendation, "Who has ears to hear, let him hear."

My final word for the reader to remember is that a Christian has all the needed ingredients within himself to become not only a mature plant, but also a fruit producing plant. Many Evangelical Christians believe those who practice Calvinism (limited atonement and election) can miss the blessing of winning others to Christ since much of their belief rests on the doctrine of election. Calvinism teaches that some people are appointed to be saved while others are destined to be lost. If a person only cares about his own maturity, he may stand in jeopardy with God. Jesus

CHAPTER THREE: PARABLE OF THE SOWER, SEEDS AND SOILS

saw a fig tree that was full of green leaves and thought it would have fruit, but upon a closer inspection, He found it bare. Therefore, He cursed the tree not only to never bear, but cursed it to die. We need to concern ourselves with our personal witness as well as our personal maturity. This may imply that, for the lack of witness, the would-be fruit would whither and die on the vine.

Please allow me to re-establish the premises of the lesson: along with prayer, the believer has a responsibility to "work out his own salvation" by removing the rocks or attitudes, mental disorders, or sin that prevents him or her from growing into a mature Christian. In addition, he must be aware of Satan's demons (birds) that are set to steal the seed. Problems and setbacks due to natural causes are part of life – they will happen to everyone. How problems are handled determines the rate of maturity and the chance to produce physical and spiritual fruit. The believer must be watchful of all types of tares that may spring up near him. As soon as a weed is discovered and determined to be a hindrance, it must be pulled from the soul or mind. The believer must become more watchful or spiritually discerning of the enemy because he will unsuspectingly sow spiritual tares that appear like harmless thoughts. They come unaware and at inopportune times when one least expects them. This type of tare could be a negative or evil thought or it could be a physical person with an evil intent placed in one's path to misdirect the work God intended for him to do.

The Christian in the pew must first see the need to rid his garden of rocks. It may be wise to name them to determine their importance so that those could be removed first. He may need a plan of attack. He may need help in determining what is more dangerous, the hidden rocks lying under the surface or the ones in plan view. The hidden rocks may be of a greater hindrance than the ones in full view. He may need assistance in their removal, only to the point of moral support and being held accountable. A friend or counselor can pray for the individual to gain strength which will enable him to see the job completed. Church attendance, reading the Bible, and praying are needful. Through these three avenues one can locate his rocks and tares that need to be removed. The same thing applies to the tares that grow naturally and those that are planted on purpose by the "wicked one." One should not beat himself up over small setbacks, or develop a guilt complex. Guilt, many times, is a major rock or at least a honeysuckle vine that will keep him tied up so tight he will be unable to move. Tending one's garden is an ongoing task. Paul instructs us to pray daily. It is just as important to keep the mind clean as it is the body. One can wash in the pool of the word or take a shower of prayer. Remember, prayer can only reveal, strengthen, or direct; it can not remove a pebble unless God wills a miracle. Life is made up of few miracles. But you can do a lot of things through Christ who will strengthen you (Phil. 4:13). The abundant Christian life comes by more hard work and sweat than miracles, but the rewards are greater than any work the believer can do. Those who were mature were encouraged by Christ to bare the burden of the weak. James concludes his letter with, "…he which convert[s] a sinner from his way shall save a soul from death and shall hide a multitude of sins." (James 5:20)

Notes:

Tim LaHaye, *The Battle for the Mind*. Old Tappan, N.J.: Fleming H. Revell Company Publishers.

Richard Strauss, *Win The Battle For Your Mind*. Neptune, N. J.: Laizeaux Bros.

Joyce Meyer, *Battlefield of the Mind*. New York: Warner Faith, 1995.

— CHAPTER FOUR —

SLEEPING SAINTS

Message Listing

Inner Preface:

Message One	Introduction to Sleeping Saints
Message Two	Sleeping During Preaching
Message Three	Sleeping During the Time of Transfiguration
Message Four	Sleeping During Prayer
Message Five	Sleeping While the Lord Tarries His Return

CHAPTER FOUR: SLEEPING SAINTS

Inner Preface for Sleeping Saints

I wish to thank two men that inspired the writing and preaching of the messages you are about to read. First, Dr. Gary Colman mentioned that many Christians were in the state of spiritual slumber in his introduction to a message he delivered while in a New England conference. The second inspiration came from Brother Cameron's article that appeared a week later in the December issue of the ***Family Altar News*** (founded by Lester Roloff), entitled "While Men Slept." Appreciation is also extended to Rev. Raymond Marchand, former medical missionary to Jordan, who proofread and typed the original manuscript.

The original message began as a typical four-point Sunday morning sermon, but the Spirit of God filled my heart with the reality that many of my fellow brothers in the Lord, like myself are preaching our hearts out to slumbering congregations. The Holy Spirit placed a burden in my soul to develop a message for each time a saint was found sleeping in scriptures in addition to an introductory sermon on the subject of sleeping saints. A few revisions have been made in this second edition. I hope that God will arouse a few

Christians and preachers alike to trumpet out the clear Gospel of Jesus Christ before this era becomes any darker with Satan's evil cloud of wickedness.

I challenge the readers, but especially pastors, to adapt these messages to their congregations. They could also serve as a month-long Bible study to spark discussion on ways to awaken your church to the reality that a number of believers in the 21st Century are not in the same realm of the 1st Century Christians. We need to get back to the belief that God is and that He is Supreme and rewards those who seek Him.

May God richly bless your endeavor as I pray for the Holy Spirit to awaken us all to the needs of the day. May God reveal Himself of His true power, grace, and forgiveness.

Chapter Four: Sleeping Saints

Message One: Introduction To Sleeping Saints

— MESSAGE ONE —

Introduction To Sleeping Saints

From the beginning God divided time. He called our basic measure of time "day." It was divided into light and dark or day and night. God further divided the day into three equal eight-hour shifts. An important shift was allocated to sleep. Sleep was a gift to rest man's body and mind during which time healing and strengthening can take place. Sick people find healing during the period of sleep; in fact, persons with high fevers are inclined to sleep more than a person who is well. A new born baby's first few days are allotted to sleep 10 ½ to 22 ½ hours. The older one becomes, the less sleep is required. Overactive people tend to sleep much less than average, but of course, excessive lack of sleep can be dangerous to one's health. If a person sleeps eight hours a day (not including naps) he will have slept 56 hours in a week. That equals to 224 hours a month; 2,912 hours a year; 188,160 hours in an average lifetime. This is equivalent to 2.3 days a week or 119 days a year. One has to wonder as to the reason humans do not accomplish anymore than they do. Frustration might add to the seemingly quiet period a person is out of commission, if we consider the time he spends before the television, computer, or sports events. Where does the time go?

People seem to be more asleep than awake these days. Some people go through their entire lives in a daze or daydream. It seems that such a person is divorcing themselves from reality. The Bible speaks of a literal and a metaphorical sleep. The New Testament speaks of sleep in five different categories. In the next few minutes we will examine these and see with which we can personally identify. First, when the word "sleep" is used in scripture, it does not always refer to death, but since we are on the subject, let us examine the sleep that resembles death.

Dead Saints Asleep in Christ

I Thessalonians 4:14: *For if we believe that Jesus died and rose again, even so them also which sleep in Jesus will God*

MESSAGE ONE: INTRODUCTION TO SLEEPING SAINTS

bring with him.

This reference refers to physical death. (Please note that this series is written from the Christian prospective – written to those who are believers in Christ.) The scripture tells us that the Christian never spiritually dies. It is the flesh alone that dies to return to dust. It should be noted that the souls of all men continues to exist. The saved believer will live in heaven with God and the Savior Jesus Christ; whereas, the lost individual's soul will exist in hell with Satan. This "lostness" can be defined as being separated from the loving and true God. The key difference is that the Christian will be reunited as a whole and living person with a new body for his spirit to live with Jesus Christ.

However, we have the curious phenomenon of living Christians who appear to be dead or perpetually asleep. They do not read the Bible; do not pray, seldom attend church, and almost never witness. Jesus states in Matthew 5:13 that the believers are to be the salt of the earth; but if this salt has lost its saltiness, it is not good for anything. Verse 14 tells the reader that the Christian should also be the light of the world. Yet, if the Christian should hide his light (influence) under a bushel basket, he exhibits the tendency of sleeping. The Apostle Paul calls such a person a "castaway." They are useless to God, and they will be held in contempt at the Judgment Seat of Christ.

Christians, who are "spiritually dead" through indolent sleeping could be the reason there has not been a significant revival in America for the last fifty years. Jesus gives life, but the stewardship of life is left to the Christian. No preacher can resurrect that which does not wish to be alive. He can not pray for them in their place nor can he read the Bible for them, etc. For the church not to die on the vine there must be life added to the body. The only way this happens is for a rebirth to take place. The first New Testament church had spiritual births on a daily basis "such as would be saved." Moreover, God sent the fire upon the altar of man's soul at the time he was born again. It is the responsibility of the believer to keep his own fire (excitement) burning as the Levitical priests had the responsibility to keep the two alters of the Tabernacle burning.

Sleeping Saints Are Carnal

I Corinthians 11:30, 31: *For this cause many [are] weak and sickly among you, and many sleep. For if we would judge ourselves, we should not be judged.*

MESSAGE ONE: INTRODUCTION TO SLEEPING SAINTS

I Corinthians 3:3: *For ye are yet carnal: for whereas [there is] among you envying, and strife, and divisions, are ye not carnal, and walk as men?*

A carnal Christian is very much, but not completely, like a dead sinner. According to Vines *Expository Dictionary of New Testament Words*, **carnal or carnally** [*sarkikoi*] is listed as "having the nature of flesh, i.e., sensual, controlled by animal appetites, governed by human nature, instead of by the Spirit of God" (p. 161).

Carnality is a preface to death as I have previously mentioned. Generally people do not die suddenly (unless death comes from a heart attack) nor are they stricken suddenly with sleep. Therefore, death and sleep of this sort becomes a process; they acquire a preceding cause of death. If someone professes Christ as Savior and there is no accompanying fruit, I personally question their spiritual birth. If there is no church attendance; no turning from sin; no obedience to Christ in being baptized, I even seriously question they are truly born again. Their action or the lack thereof goes against the definition of being a new creature in Christ. Pastors and Christians alike do not wish to mention this doctrinal truth for fear it may offend someone, mainly the lost. But are we truthful to God's word by not holding one accountable for his or her profession of faith? Who knows – if we compassionately reveal the reality of hell, the individual in question could decide to accept Jesus as Savior (with the wooing of the Holy Spirit) instead of becoming more offensive.

I understand that there is a period of time allowed for a new Christian to develop growth. Most pastors allow for this, and I am sure God knows all about this period since He equated being born again with the birth of babies and the need of milk to begin the process toward maturity, (1 Peter 2:2). Paul wrote in his letter to the Galatians, *"If we live in the Spirit let us also walk in the Spirit"* (5:16-18). It is very easy to say one is a Christian and on the way to heaven; however, if one lives as if he were hell bound, he must expect a firm "No" to another's perceptions as to whether one reads the Bible, prays, or attends church.

Why not test yourself? In a minute's time, without prior thought, list ten things you enjoy doing. Is there anything about God among the ten items? Ask yourself these questions: "Would Jesus do what I am doing, or would God be glorified in what I am doing?" These are urgent questions.

MESSAGE ONE: INTRODUCTION TO SLEEPING SAINTS

Sleeping Saints Are Insensitive To Sin

Romans 13:11-14: *And that, knowing the time, that now [it is] high time to awake out of sleep: for now [is] our salvation nearer than when we believed. The night is far spent, the day is at hand: let us therefore cast off the works of darkness, and let us put on the armor of light. Let us walk honestly, as in the day; not in rioting and drunkenness, not in chambering and wantonness, not in strife and envying. But put ye on the Lord Jesus Christ, and make not provision for the flesh, to [fulfill] the lusts [thereof].*

Works of darkness are works of sin. The Bible tells us to put on the armor of light. As long as there is light, darkness is excluded. One light in a room stops the outside darkness at the windows. The brighter we glow for the Lord, the further darkness retreats.

Ask yourself another question; "Does sin bother you?" Or do you reason that everyone is doing it in order to cast aside the convicting or grieving Spirit in consequence? Do you say with the comic, "The devil made me do it?" Be assured that the devil can only do what man allows or permits him to do. Once the devil is invited into your life, it becomes very difficult to get rid of him. But it is possible to expel the demonic influence because Christ is truly the stronger of the two. Let us not forget the words of James 4:7: "Resist the devil and he will flee from you."

Conversely, is there sorrow, humility, or an attempt at correcting your action when you realize you have sinned? Do you know what sin is? Do you know sin drains the power and light from you; that it spoils the saltiness; that it grieves and quenches the Holy Spirit (who is one's only sure and holy power supply)? If someone points out sin to you, do you laugh it off? Do you become angry? Are you offended by this reminder without first examining its validity? More concretely, do you stop attending church or merely seek another church just because the pastor happened to mention your private sin in a message?

Too many Christians are like the poor frog that was placed in cold water on the stove. The frog does not realize that the water is becoming hotter and hotter until the water has boiled and the frog is cooked. The devil is subtle. He does not come on strong enough to scare man away from sin, but rather slowly and deceitfully reintroduces sin in the person's life until sin becomes his life. This can happen to any Christian, especially if he is sleeping. Sleeping saints are carnal and insensitive to sin. Moreover...

Sleeping Saints Are Unconcerned

I Thessalonians 5:5, 6: *Ye are all the children of light, and the children of the day: we are not of the night, nor of darkness. Therefore let us not sleep, as [do] others; but let us watch and be sober.*

The Saints of God who are fast asleep tend to be unconcerned that the Lord Jesus is soon returning. This is exactly the opposite of what today's Christians are looking for, and this attitude is totally out of keeping with the expectant attitude of Christ's disciples and that of the early church. Many present-day Christians are so unconcerned over the second coming that they take their unconcern to extremes. They are almost incurably "at rest." They perform virtually no service at all in the expectation of Christ's return for His church.

Worse! These sleeping saints are quite *comfortable* living in the flesh and being part of the world. They have no desire to change their lives in any way and care far too little for the perfect heavenly life – both the literal heavenly life, and the life here on earth colored by heaven's holy society. In fact, the list of things with which they are unconcerned is almost endless: church attendance, the state of their city, the state of the world they emulate, unrest, the condition of the lost, etc., *ad infinitum*. Truly, there seems to be no concern. They have their fabricated excuses, however. Foremost among their alibis are the shabby lives of other Christians. They consider hypocrisy to be an original discovery, little realizing that they are allowing the very dregs of Christianity to set their spiritual pace. It is always sad whenever one seeks out the very lowest existing standard to emulate.

Such sleeping Christians are unconcerned over the church's mission to send evangelists – whether at home, within the realm of their own responsibilities, or around the world at large through missionaries. It is always been God's plan to build, yet they could care less. "Why is the house of God forsaken?" questioned, Nehemiah (13:11). There are more questions to be asked: Why do we live in finished houses, shutting ourselves away from the world like monks and hermits? Why do we forsake any and all church work? Why have we broken down the walls of the distinctive Christian life to live among that which is rubbish? (Neh.

MESSAGE ONE: INTRODUCTION TO SLEEPING SAINTS

4:10). It is all a result of an almost hypnotic spiritual sleep.
Sleeping Saints Cannot Hear the Message of God

Acts 20: 6-12: *And upon the first [day] of the week, when the disciples came together to break bread, Paul preached unto them, ready to depart on the morrow; and continued his speech until midnight. And there were many lights in the upper chamber, where they were gathered together. And there sat in a window a certain young man named Eutychus, being fallen into a deep sleep: and as Paul was long preaching*, **he sunk down with sleep, and fell down from the third loft, and was taken up dead** [My emphasis]. *And Paul went down, and fell on him, and embracing [him] said, Trouble not yourselves; for his life is in him. When he therefore was come up again, and had broken bread, and eaten, and talked a long while, even till break of day, so he departed. And they brought the young man alive, and were not a little comforted*

It would be amazing and at the most an outright scandal if what was on the minds of a given church congregation were known to all. The average church member is in another world mentally [I have found my mind wondering several times during service.] "I wonder if I will get that bank loan. How are my kids going to have the life they deserve? Is my wife faithful? Does my spouse know that I have a wandering eye? What will we have for dinner today? I wonder if John Doe will annoy us with another Sunday visit? When does that ball game start? Rats! I wish the preacher would not raise his voice like he does to make his point; is there a real need for that? What Christian has not thought, "Paul had lengthy messages, but perhaps he had something of substance to say; if this preacher keeps going on and on, I will miss my favorite afternoon movie." Sound familiar? This mental wandering comes from the irrelevant, disconnected thoughts of spiritual sleep.

How do you react when God uses a message to speak to your heart? Do you become angry? Do you just ignore the message? Do you take the arrogant step of consigning the message to someone else rather than yourself? Do you even hear the message at all? Are you willing to obey God and amend your way of life, or are you totally dedicated to sleeping?

If God spoke to you, would you hear Him, or would you, too, continue sleeping? If God chose to so speak to you this very moment, would you be insensitive to your own sin and remain unconcerned? Are you so far from God as to not recognize the voice of the Spirit as young Samuel was? Have you deafened yourself to the extent of losing your Christian light and life to the point of death? Have you become so carnal or backslidden you no longer respond to God's call?

If God has spoken to you in any way, do something attentive and different: let God know that He is speaking to a living soul. Let Him know that you hear His voice. Maybe you are so very fast asleep that you even wonder if you are a true Christian. If this is so, and you feel or know that you are lost, WAKE UP! Come to Christ who with open arms is ready to receive. If you are unsure that you are a born again Christian, come to Him by claiming Romans 10:9 in faith and He will save you and give you assurance of a heavenly home today!

Notes:

W. E. Vine, MA, *An Expository Dictionary of New Testament Words*. Nashville, TN: Thomas Nelson Publishers.

CHAPTER FOUR: SLEEPING SAINTS

— MESSAGE TWO —

SLEEPING DURING PREACHING

Acts 20:6-12: [9] *And there sat in a window a certain young man named Eutychus, being fallen into a deep sleep: and as Paul was long preaching, he sunk down with sleep, and fell down from the third loft, and was taken up dead.*

This message, like the other ones in this volume, is not necessarily directed toward the lost person, but rather toward the Christian believer. As a matter of fact, the Bible was not written for the express purpose of reaching the lost. Its chief target is the Christian since the words are said to be spiritual. It takes a spiritual person (having the indwelling Spirit of God) to fully understand what God is trying to teach His child. Of the 39 books of the Old Testament most of them are meant to be examples to believers. Of the 27 books of the New Testament, twenty-one deal with spiritual growth. The four Gospels tell the story of Jesus; the Book of Acts shows the birth of the church and the Book of Revelation reveals the end-times. This leaves 21 books that instruct the believer how he or she should live a Christian life.

If a person has never read the Scriptures over an extended period of time and/or was unable to understand the simplest biblical teaching, there is a great possibility that individual would be unable to include him or herself among those who proclaim to be born again. I would examine the heart deeply and honestly to determine the kind of relationship that person had with God, if any. Many people come so close; yet, miss the true meaning of salvation. They miss the essential meaning of being transformed from a kingdom of darkness into the kingdom of light. Many people know only the language of salvation or orthodox Christianity. They have fallen into Satan's most subtle trap: the ability to cloud the mind with empty words that lack the reality necessary to assure them of their true salvation.

Today Christians need to WAKE UP! Cry aloud!

Clap your hands and even stomp your feet if needed (Ezekiel 6:11) to get the sleeper's attention. In addition, we need to tear down and root up old philosophies that have caused the church to drop off into slumber. Do anything but assume the standard Christian posture of holding down a pew with one's dignity. *The stouthearted are spoiled, they have slept their sleep: and none of the men of might have found their hands. At thy rebuke, O God of Jacob, both the chariot and horse are cast into a dead sleep* (Psalms 76:5, 6). We need to gain the attention of the lost world because it is running headlong toward the oblivious pit of destruction. We cannot use prayer as the sole vehicle to get men to heaven. The individual himself must turn from the broad way that leads to destruction into the narrow way leading to everlasting life. He is in need of a guide that is not asleep and who knows the way.

For decades, it appears as if a subtle drowsiness and a spiritual stupor have settled down upon the vast majority of professing Christians. It is almost impossible to arouse them to a wide-eyed, full consciousness of the alarming and perilous condition of Christendom.

Sleeping During the Preaching Service (Acts 20: 9)

Chapter Four: Sleeping Saints

Some people literally sleep their lives through while attending church. They are too tired to remain physically awake; they are too bored with *dead services*; and/or they are just not interested in spiritual matters. Never mind their being concerned over others; they are not concerned enough over themselves to remain conscious. In the same instance pastors need to preach with enough compassion and urgency to keep the congregation awake and motivated enough to contend for the faith. People complain that there is not enough action in the church services. Such "believers" may come to church to be entertained. Others may complain that the preacher fails to fill his message with enough levity. Others may sleep with the profound overconfidence in the belief that the church will always be open and available for anyone who may wonder inside. Should a given church close her doors for the lack of attendance, (for hundreds of churches close their doors daily) it would hardly faze the average church attendee at all. They would think nothing of going elsewhere to sleep through another service.

What would be the effect upon the nation if all gospel-preaching churches were forced to close their doors? There are evil powers at work that are denying the existence of a Supreme Being, especially if it has any resemblance to

MESSAGE TWO: SLEEPING DURING PREACHING

Christianity. America has become pluralistic by accepting all faiths and beliefs. What would you do if your pastor no longer preached a biblical message? What would you do if your church adopted a more liberal philosophy; would you know the difference? Would you have a strong enough faith and knowledge to read your Bible and pray at home? Could you teach you own children the love of God and what is required of a true believer? That day may be closer than you wish to admit or visualize.

We send our children to school for twelve years to learn the "Three Rs"; yet, it seems that we expect the same students to learn and understand all spiritual aspects of God intuitively by spending only two hours between Sunday school and worship service. Is this not a faulty expectation? We will not learn unless we are taught; and we will not be teachable unless faith is present. This faith comes only by hearing the word of God; and where do we hear if not at church. Besides, we need to stay awake along enough to hear the message.

There are those who manage to sleep soundly yet remain technically awake – they daydream throughout the message and never look at the scripture text that is being use. We need to PAY ATTENTION!! Wake up! Look alive and take note of what is being said. Matthew wrote in 13:25: *But while they slept his enemy came and sowed tares among the wheat.* Satan wishes to choke out the real gospel that is able to set people free of all form of bondage.

Spiritual Sleep

Revelation 2:1-3:22: illustrates spiritual sleep through the seven letters to the churches.

There is an epidemic of acute spiritual exhaustion in our churches these days. (See the final essay, *An Analogy of Spiritual Anemia*.) It is almost as if we had a total spiritual vacuum. We are functioning on all planes but the spiritual. We depend upon our labor because we understand the necessity of having money. Some depend upon welfare or some other program supported by the government to supply all their needs while others look to their neighbors to help them through difficult times. Hardly anyone relies upon prayer any longer. This in itself is a clinical symptom of spiritual digress. The Bible warns us that people will wax colder as the days of apostasy become more prevalent. Christians today wish to be spoon fed with things sweet –

not with anything that will promote change. They do not wish to "study to show themselves approved into God." Consequently, Christians are being swept into cults, sects, errors, tolerance, political correctness, and just plain lies of Satan. Christianity, as a whole, has been asleep so long that the philosophies of humanism and materialism have taken a foothold in the church; thus, supplanting true beliefs. It is as if man has achieved a kind of superior "god-ship," wherein the mind of the average believer has become a judge of God's actions.

The letters to the seven churches that are found in the Book of Revelation seem to prove the fact that Christians will appear to be more asleep in the days ahead than ever before. We are presently seeing the preliminary consequences of this sleep unfolding before our eyes. Sleepers do not notice error and liberalism slipping into the church, nor do the prechers themselves appear alert or aware enough of what their flock is doing, studying, or to the fact they are asleep in the pews. Let us examine the seven churches found in the Book of Revelation to determine if Christ could be warning the present generation of possible consequences of spiritual slumber.

CHAPTER FOUR: SLEEPING SAINTS

The Church at Ephesus: Revelation 2:1-7

The church at Ephesus slept soundly enough to ignore and lose her first love, namely Jesus Christ. Actually the people *"left"* their first love. The leaving was done on purpose. This neglect has its appropriate judgment: their candlestick was to be removed, if their slumber continued. In other words the power and the presence of God will be taken from this type of church, if correction is not made. But God so loved this church He allowed enough time for her to repent in order to escape loosing her spiritual essence.

The Church at Smyrna: Revelation 2:8-11

The Smyrna church historically had continuing unresolved problems, yet remained faithful among the trials. People encountering a Smyrna-type church increased their faith. Church members do not leave a Bible preaching church simply due to slight imperfections. While there are one or two biblical reasons for leaving a given church, in my many years in the ministry, I have yet to see anyone leave the church I was pastoring for a biblical reason. Usually they leave because a given problem disturbs their sleep or demands that they awaken enough to apply themselves to solving the problem. Not willing to be aroused enough to correct their Christian walk, the weakened believers commit an even greater sin by falling by the wayside; thus, causing a break or further weakness in the line of defense.

The Church at Pergomos: Revelation 2:12-17

The Pergomos church, in the midst of its sleep cycle, picked up the doctrine of Balaam, i.e.. putting aside true doctrine, faith, and knowledge for the mere sake of gain or personal advantage. A church like the one at Pergomos places stumbling blocks before fellow Christians, i.e., they construct impediments to hinder the maturity of their brothers and sisters. Like the Old Testament Pharisees, they specialize in adding burdens to others. Whether or not they are members of a sound Bible church, you can count upon a Pergomos-type church person to hinder others who love the truth itself, and who wish to grow in grace. Such sleepers also relish the opportunity to teach others to partake of sinful things and water down their allegiance to God by adding worldly standards or habits to their life style. Jesus pronounced a judgment for this type of church: *Repent; or else I will come unto thee quickly, and will fight against them with the sword of my mouth"* (Revelation 2:16).

The Church at Thyatira: Revelation 2:18-29

The Thyatiran church was where the men sleep; therefore, allowed women to fill their rightful place as designed by God. A modern Thyatira church would be prone to allow a television heretic to influence their dreams in order that they could continue to exist on the sleeping pills of heresy and false doctrine. For those that overdose, there is a judgment: *And I gave her space to repent of her fornication; and she repented not. Behold, I will cast her into a bed, and them that commit adultery with her into great tribulation, except they repent of their deeds. And I will kill her children with death; and all the churches shall know that I am he which [searches] the reins and hearts: and I will give unto every one of you according to your works* (vs. 21-23).

The Church at Sardis Revelation 3:1-6

The church at Sardis believed that spiritual sleep was perfectly acceptable as long as one is saved. The members did not realize the possibility there were others sitting in the pews beside them who needed to be saved. The salvation that Christ gives is not private or exclusive property. Members of such a church must watch that their sinful sleep does not invade the home or neighborhood. One's salvation does not permit him or her to sit in slumber while the family or community teeters toward hell. Such a slothful and selfish sleep will be judged: *Remember therefore how thou hast received and heard, and hold fast, and repent. If therefore thou [will] not watch, I will come on thee as a thief, and thou [will] not know what hour I will come upon thee,* (v. 3).

The Church at Philadelphia: Revelation 3:7-13

The church at Philadelphia, even though faithful and vigilant, had a slumbering problem that allowed the unsaved to become part of the congregation. We need to test professing Christians in order to determine who produced their fruit – the Holy Spirit or was an unclean spirit responsible for their fruit. If they are not saved, the Holy Spirit can only influence them to be saved but not to grow. Life must first be given before any growth is possible. We are, therefore, encouraged in 1 John 4:1: *Not to believe every spirit, but to try the spirits whether they are of God* or not. The answer to why is found in 1Timothy 4:1: *...in the latter times some shall depart from the faith, giving heed to seducing spirits, and doctrines of devils.* One will soon notice the absence of power, the lack of inner peace, and an unforgiving spirit. Conversely, such will have a bitter and rebellious attitude. If they remain unsaved, such people will be the first to cause problems in the church and the first to leave the church over matters of little consequence. A member of a Philadelphia-type church must be extra careful to remain alert and awake. More is always expected of the steadfast and the faithful.

The Church at Laodicea: **Revelation 3:14-22**

The Laodicean church is the absolute "pits" of all churches; the worse of the seven. Members of such a church are so asleep that they can not distinguish between hot and cold, but know only a tepid lukewarm temperature that allows them to discern nothing spiritual. If you have met such church people; they are the ones who will do anything but offend anyone. They would never rock the boat. Despite whatever abominable heresies are bandied about, the members of this church remain neutral, non-offensive, politically correct, and tolerant of all beliefs regardless of their doctrine. Members of a Laodicean congregation are sleeping so soundly that they will allow their fruit (if any) to rot. They are advocates of sleep. I do not adhere "going to the church of your choice." Because of immaturity, a person may choose a wrong place of worship where the gospel is not preached. The Laodicean-type church allows its members to believe and practice any variety of doctrines. The view that everyone, saved or lost, are God's children is unbiblical.

Most parents would not trust just anyone to care for their children. References would be checked in regards of dependability and responsibility. The person who leads another to salvation is responsible for the proper diet, growth, and training of the said person, which will lead to his or her maturity. The average person would not rescue a child from drowning merely to send him on his way without seeing that he arrived home safely. The soul winner's duty does not stop at salvation. The Good Samaritan (Luke 10:30-37) did not leave the wounded man on the side of the road. He took him personally to the innkeeper, i.e., pastor, who provided shelter for rest and food for healing and instruction. The Samaritan also paid a "tithe" for whatever expense might be required to house the individual. The reader should note that the rescuer would be returning to check on the progress of his new found friend.

Once a person is saved, it is a sin to stay away from church regardless of the reason (Hebrews 12:25). A renewed church attendance is a good sign of a proper salvation. People of a Laodicean-type church are in peril due to their dedication to spiritual sleep and apathy. Their judgment is severe. They are viewed in such a bad light that they make Jesus vomit. In lieu of their lackadaisical attitude and spiritual sleep, the Laodiceans think well of themselves; but in truth, they are poor, miserable, wretched, naked, and blind.

Satan's Mist of Sleep Hinders Christian Influence

When a Christian sleeps, chances are that he or she will miss the excitement of preaching. Preaching is a chosen instrument of God to get His message of love to the world. We all need to awaken to the "Amens!" Wake up and be glad you are saved. If you even suspect you are becoming drowsy, force a wake up call! Shake yourself awake or ask someone to splash you with the truth from God's word. One should get a good night sleep before church service, not during the service.

Strange things happen to sleeping saints. They cannot be encouraged to read the Scriptures; they cannot be instructed in sound doctrine; they cannot be instructed in simple daily Christian living; nor can the sleeper be reproved or corrected to live a better and richer life. Sleeping saints will miss important things in life, like the joy of seeing others saved. They behave as if they are spiritually dead rather than merely sleeping. Sleepers appear unconcerned over their neighbors or even their own personal spiritual

Message Two: Sleeping During Preaching

relationship, and growth, or maturity.

Without being saved, no sin is subtracted from one's account; thus, "the wages of sin is death and separation from God." Once a person seals his or her fate by rejecting Christ, he or she falls under God's judgment and pays the penalty of being consumed eternally in the Lake of Fire – the place of outer and inner darkness with unquenchable flames. In such a place the individual who laughed and scoffed at God and His church and His saints will be rudely and forcefully awakened never to sleep again.

The sleepers will be cast fully awake into the Lake of Fire prepared for the devil and his angels (Matthew 25:41). They will always remember the times they slept through Sunday service. They were asleep when their loved ones and friends tried to witness to them about the hideous place known as hell. In that day, they will wish for a single instant when they could close their eyes to the burning fires about them. They will likewise wish that their ears could again be deafened in sleep so as not to hear the everlasting shrieks and tormented cries of others around them who are experiencing the same fate. They will crave the gentle, kind slumber of sleep that could deaden the pain of their burning souls. They will wish that a refreshing sleep would take hold of them to enable their minds to forget the innumerable times their loved ones, the preacher, or wives or husbands, or even their children begged them to be saved.

My friends do not sleep your own souls or the souls of your loved ones into hell; for the lack of witness. Do not sleep your city into hell or your church into apostasy. AWAKE! Cry out! Cry aloud! Spare nothing for sleep will be snatched away, the disillusioned mist of Satan will be lifted, and the burning darkness of hell will become a stark reality.

Are you sleeping or daydreaming in church? Are you sleeping when a man of God delivers the message from God? Are you contentedly sleeping while your city goes to hell? Wake up! Wake up, before it is too late and before the hands of time stop or before the last grain of sand falls in the hourglass. Rather, work while it still day. There is a time coming when no one will be able to witness freely. The door of salvation will be closing in the near future (Matthew 25:10-13). We should pray for power, wisdom, and for tears for the lost – remembering all the while, "It is a fearful thing to fall into the hands of an angry God." (Hebrews 10:31)

— MESSAGE THREE —

SLEEPING DURING THE TIME OF TRANSFIGURATION

Luke 9: 28-36: *And it came to pass about an eight days after these sayings, he took Peter and John and James, and went up into a mountain to pray. And as he prayed, the fashion of his countenance was altered, and his raiment [was] white [and] glistering. And, behold, there talked with him two men, which were Moses and Elias: Who appeared in glory, and spake of his decease which he should accomplish at Jerusalem. But Peter and they that were with him were heavy with sleep: and when they were awake, they saw his glory, and the two men that stood with him. And it came to pass, as they departed from him, Peter said unto*

Chapter Four: Sleeping Saints

Jesus, Master, it is good for us to be here: and let us make three tabernacles; one for thee, and one for Moses, and one for Elias: not knowing what he said. While he thus spake, there came a cloud, and overshadowed them: and they feared as they entered into the cloud. And there came a voice out of the cloud, saying, This is my beloved Son: hear him. And when the voice was past, Jesus was found alone. And they kept [it] close, and told no man in those days any of those things which they had seen.

Jesus again separated Peter, James, and John and taught them privately. These men were to be the inner circle of the church: the future leaders. Jesus had gone up a mountain to pray. We often learn by the prayers of others, and we should remember God answers many times while we are praying. By missing prayer time, all too many miss the blessings of God. When you miss the time of prayer at church, you may miss the outpouring of God's power. Jesus intended that these three men have a true "mountain top experience."

Nevertheless, this set of Apostles missed the actual transformation of Jesus because their eyes were "heavy with sleep." The men just could not keep their eyes open; thus, they fell into a deep sleep, at which time, the countenance of

MESSAGE THREE: SLEEPING DURING THE TIME OF TRANSFIGURATION

Jesus changed. He took upon Himself His future glorified state that would be seen at His resurrection and second coming. What a sight it would have been for the Apostles to witness their Lord's change. Luke's word describing this event was "glistening, meaning new; dazzling, or having to do with intense light, or to bring about brilliance and splendor." It is note worthy to point out that Luke does not use the word, "transfigure," but Matthew and Mark do. Matthew used the Greek word, *me-ta-mor-phoo*, meaning "to change into another form." It is where we get the word metamorphosis. It implies a complete change of form and appearance, much like when a caterpillar changes into a butterfly. Luke implies that a true change occurred that showed His future radiant state, i.e., His celestial body. Briefly, Jesus dropped His humanity to reveal how He would appear in Glory. This also gives us an idea how a believer's body will appear in heaven because the Scripture tells us that we will be like Him.

In researching for this message I thought it to be phenomenal, after checking several volumes of sermons of American preachers, that I was unable to find a single message on Christ's Transfiguration. In fact, I have only heard it mentioned in passing as an illustration; no single message has been located/devoted to the text in question. There are a number of unique things about Luke's record that need to be considered. First, there is the occurrence of a set of threes: (a) the three Apostles; (b) Christ and the two visitors equal three; (c) Peter wanted to build three tabernacles. Then there is the item that the same three Apostles were singled out on three different occasions: at the house of Jairus, here on the mountain, and again at the Garden of Gethsemane. We also have the second time that God the Father speaks: first at the baptism of Jesus and in this text when He speaks from the cloud. Something that should be further considered is the absence of angels. The heavenly beings are seen following the temptation of Christ to strengthen the Messiah. Following the three-fold prayer of Jesus, angels were sent again to strengthen Him. Hence, what is the reason behind the absence of the spiritual assistance at this time? The answer could be that Jesus wished to assure the Apostles who He was. If so, God does not share His glory with anyone or anything. This is the reason Peter's request to build three shrines was ignored. Even though Moses and Elijah were great men, they were not deity.

The question must be asked as to the purpose of the appearance of Moses and Elijah? It could be to prove there is life after death. Jesus stated that Jehovah was the God of the living not the dead. Then there is the presence of prayer that needs to be considered. Moses and Elijah as well as Christ were all men of prayer. Please note that it was only Luke that recognizes or records every time Jesus prayed in particular. Verse twenty-nine says, *And as he prayed, the fashion of his countenance was altered....* Out the four Gospels it was Luke that mentions that Jesus prayed during His baptism. The three Synoptics recorded the choosing of the twelve Apostles, but only Luke shows Jesus praying before choosing His future preachers. Again it is only Luke that mentions that Christ prayed during His crucifixion, Father *forgive them for they know not what they do....*

My personal question is: "How did the Apostles know the two men were Moses and Elijah, and why were these particular men present? First, each man may have been dressed a particular way as to identify who he was or they may have carried something that would have set them apart from other Bible characters. Second, it may have been that Moses stood alone against a rebellious and backslidden people of his day. Likewise, Elijah stood against the principalities and powers of a devil-inspired governmental system. And Christ was soon to make the greatest stand in history: a stand against sin. Perhaps Moses and Elijah were chosen because they were mountain men: Moses spent time upon Mt. Sinai; Elijah had a battle on Mt. Carmel, and Jesus had three mountains in His life, Mount of Temptation, Mount of Transfiguration, and Mount Calvary. Finally, it may have been because of the requests of the two men. Moses asked to see the Glory of God; and Elijah called fire from the sky. Jesus was then seen in His glorified state for Moses and for Elijah. Jesus would later state, *"I am come to bring fire upon the earth,"* (Luke 12:49).

Because Peter, James, and John were sleeping, they missed witnessing the process of change. It is like missing the development of a bolt of cloth into a suit; or the evolution of a painting from a blank canvas into a finished work of art. Permit me to ask another question, "Would you like to go to sleep one night and awake to find yourself ten years into the future with your children grown?" No, of course not! Most people would like to see the gentle process or the transformation from youth to adulthood.

There is a definite spiritual parallel. Sleeping Christians hazard finding those spiritually younger than themselves suddenly more mature than themselves. They hazard the total loss of complete ministries. They suddenly

MESSAGE THREE: SLEEPING DURING THE TIME OF TRANSFIGURATION

awaken without memory like an amnesiac. They awaken to their spouse full of life, talent, and being blessed of God, while they still struggle to digest spiritual milk.

Not only did the Apostles miss things by sleeping, the prophets and preachers (past and present) have also missed important events. Moses, the great law giver, and Elijah, the prophet, were in the last leg of their departure when the three sleepers awoke only in time to catch the last few seconds of them being taken away. The Apostles would have been an unmatched blessing if they overheard the final conversations Moses and Elijah had with Jesus. How much more powerful and affective would have the Apostles been because of the content they would have heard?

Let us look at Luke's account of the transfiguration again. The two prophets discussed Jesus' death or decease. Did you ever ask yourself the reason? Certainly it was because the very reason Christ came to earth in the first place was to die. They may have wondered what His death would accomplish. This is the core of the **Good News or Gospel**: the death, burial, and resurrection of Jesus Christ. The basic fact that Christianity emphasizes the death of its founder while other religions stress the life of their founders sets Christianity apart from all other religions. Furthermore, the reality of a living God is essential to salvation itself. *And as Moses lifted up the serpent in the wilderness even so must the Son of man be lifted up* (John 3:14). To save the children of Israel from poison snakes, Moses instructed Aaron to fasten a brazen serpent upon a stake and raise it high enough so all the people could see it. To save mankind from the poison bite of sin, Jesus had to be lifted up to hang upon a cross.

Had the Apostles been alert on the Mount of Transfiguration, they might have over- heard the two giants of faith discussing the meaning of Christ's death. They might have seen it for what it really was – a vicarious death where one suffered and died in another's place. Christ took the horrible punishment of death and spiritual separation from the Father so that we might not have to be separated from the Father. They might have anticipated Christ's death as a death that satisfied the justice of God. Sin had been committed; therefore, transgression had to be accounted for.

Fully recognizing man's inability to pay for his own sin, Jesus was appointed before the foundation of the world to make that payment out of love and mercy. He fully satisfied the absolute, moral, and holy law of God. Whereas, sin breaks the commandment of God, but the love of God dictates a healing of the breach and restoration of the sinner who broke God's law. Humankind needed an exogenous agent to make it as though Adam and his descendants had never sinned! Consequently, Christ's death was a death of ransom. His death fully paid the price of sin. Adam's seed could now be redeemed back to God. The cost of the free gift of salvation and forgiveness demanded by the Father was the death His only Begotten Son.

Another important factor of the transfiguration experience must not be overlooked: the appearance of Moses and Elijah with the transfigured Christ shouts the fact of life after death and the grave. Moses and Elijah were ALIVE! Friends, there is no such thing as "soul sleep." Adherers of this doctrine believe that the soul and flesh are one and the same. Hence, they teach that the soul of man lays in the grave with the flesh and bones until the resurrection. Consequently, those who hold to this teaching do not have assurance of salvation; on the contrary, most of the ones that I have met are unsure that they will be resurrected unto life everlasting, especially the Jehovah Witnesses. Thankfully the scripture teaches otherwise.

CHAPTER FOUR: SLEEPING SAINTS

We have other testimonies to this fact. The prophet Samuel, after his demise, appeared and talked with King Saul. Chapter sixteen in the Gospel of Luke carries the account of Lazarus and the rich man and Abraham; all these appear to be in some kind of conscious state while their bodies were lying in the grave. Finally, we have the testimony of Jesus Himself that Jehovah is the God of Abraham, Isaac, and Jacob; therefore, He is not the God of the dead, but rather, is the God of the living. For the believer, death is only a setting aside of the flesh. Death is actually the beginning of a new life. Alas! For the unbeliever physical death is the beginning of eternal torment. The "whosoever will may come" is the only way to escape the second death. The spiritual death is also known as the second death. Matthew recorded in (25:41) where the unbeliever will end up: *Then shall he say also unto them on the left hand, Depart from me, ye cursed, into everlasting fire, prepared for the devil and his angels.* This also shows that the soul of man is not totally destroyed since angels also are ever-existing spiritual beings. I would like to point out the created place by the name of hell is different from the earthly grave. The grave keeps the body and hell holds the soul.

By awakening after the fact of the transfiguration, the Apostles were at a loss as to what to do or say, and of course, erred. They said and did the wrong thing. Nothing is more conducive to error and apostasy than good sound sleep.

The Apostle's Response

Peter said, *"It is good for us to be here."* It might well have been better if he had not slept through most of the account. He then said, *Let us build three tabernacles, one for Thee, one for Moses, and one for Elijah; not knowing [or understanding] what he said.* This would be a typical comment from one first awakening from sleep. One doesn't have all his senses or mental alertness upon first awakening. Imagine equating Christ, the Creator, with His creatures. Never mind the good intensions Peter meant it to be. The man who reached out to steady the Ark of the Covenant on the cart meant well, but he did something wrong that required his life. Even the Priests could not touch the Ark with human hands. They were to use staves on either side to lift and transport the Holy Mercy Seat and Ark of the Covenant from one place to another. If David had used the correct form of transportation, the Ark would not have become unsteady. If the Apostles had remained awake, they may not have said what they said. The Bible tells us that we will be held accountable for every idle word that we utter, and especially all the bad words. It would have been better for Peter to have remained silent, but his mind was clouded by his recent sleep.

Do not diminish Peter's error. When God, the Father spoke from the cloud, He said, *This is My Beloved Son, Hear ye Him.* The Father never wanted man to even approach the idea that salvation could be by any other means but Jesus Christ. Prophets or preachers can not save a single soul. They only bring out what revelation or divine truth has been made known already. The law of God, though holy and perfect, can not save. Its very perfection stands in the way. We learn from James that it is impossible to keep the law and from Paul's letter to the Galatians we learn salvation does not come by keeping the law. *Knowing that a man is not justified by the works of the law,* (Galatians 2:16). The believer's salvation comes through faith (Ephesians 2:8, 9) and not from keeping the law. The other two tabernacles that Peter wished to build placed equal emphases in the law (Moses) and the teachings of the prophets (Elijah). Peter's proclamation stood further in error by breaking the First Commandment, *Have no other Gods before Me.* God does not share worship or His glory!

Have you ever considered what you may miss when you sleep in church or out of church? You miss several transforming miracles and the means by which they are affected. Transforming a sinner into a new creature by God's

Message Three: Sleeping During The Time Of Transfiguration

grace is a miracle; transforming a spiritual goat into a sheep is a miracle, Think too, what you missed when you slept during the Sunday evening service or during the mid-week prayer meeting. What truths were missed? How many personal revelations will go un-noticed? Thomas completely missed the first appearance of the Lord following His resurrection. Where was he? Will you miss the outpouring of the Spirit of God on your pastor or upon another Saint of God by sleeping at home or in service? Will you be totally oblivious of the presence of the Holy Spirit in the church service? Should Heaven open and pour out a blessing upon all who are in attendance; should scores be saved; should the sick and infirm be uplifted; or should the church be empowered as never before and revival brake out – you would miss it because you were sleeping. Your cup would not be filled or your basket overflowing with rich blessings because such heavenly riches are not given by proxy.

In other words, would you repeat the mistake of Peter, James, and John by sleeping when you ought to be alert and alive to God's word and possible blessings? Even today many Christians are asleep. They have slept in the past and continue napping presently. However, you need not consign the future to slumber, ask God to give you zeal, boldness, concern, and the burden to remain awake. It is a known fact the flesh is weak; therefore, we should be prepared to strengthen the weak areas. God is calling for Saints to stand the test of purposeful awareness. He is saying, "I want to bless you, I want to show you many things; I want to open the windows of heaven and bless you and yours." But for all that to happen there must be an alert church and people; those who are conscious enough to know a blessing when it comes.

Let us pray: *Dear Lord God, awake us with Your gentle touch. We need to be awaken to our spiritual needs and the needs of others. Send the Holy Spirit to make us aware that our community is ready for harvesting. Awake the lost to their need to salvation, then send your church to walk down the lanes and highways where scores of souls may be redeemed. Once we have been made aware of Your presence, let us (the church body) be receptive to the call of the Spirit in whatever area of service, Dear Lord, we yield to your direction, attune our hearing to heaven's still small voice .*
  In Jesus' name, Amen.

— MESSAGE FOUR —

SLEEPING DURING PRAYER

Matthew 26:36-45: *Then cometh Jesus with them unto a place called Gethsemane, and saith unto the disciples, Sit ye here, while I go and pray yonder. And he took with him Peter and the two sons of Zebedee, and began to be sorrowful and very heavy. Then saith he unto them, My soul is exceeding sorrowful, even unto death: tarry ye here, and watch with me. And he went a little further, and fell on his face, and prayed, saying, O my Father, if it be possible, let this cup pass from me: nevertheless not as I will, but as thou [wilt]. And he cometh unto the disciples, and findeth them asleep, and saith unto Peter, What, could ye not watch with me one hour?* **Watch and pray**,*[my emphasis] that ye enter not into temptation: the spirit indeed [is] willing, but the flesh [is] weak. He went away again the second time, and prayed....*

Chapter Four: Sleeping Saints

And he came and found them asleep again: for their eyes were heavy. And he left them, and went away again, and prayed the third time, saying the same words. Then cometh he to his disciples, and saith unto them, Sleep on now, and take [your] rest: behold, the hour is at hand, and the Son of man is betrayed into the hands of sinners. KJV

In the past chapter, the reader learned something about the Church, Christianity, and mankind. If there is one thing that Satan hates, it is for a believer to get excited about the ministry of Christ and about evangelism in particular. This includes saving souls and the preaching the gospel. Satan subtlety has become a "sandman" who has scattered a spiritual sleep among believers, imposing upon them a ghostly slumber. A silent fog of darkness has fallen upon the church to obscure her eyes from the bitter realities of danger, harm, and the need to be active in both the physical and the spiritual realms. There is a need to sound an alarm to awaken the church in order to give her time to prepare for the battle that lies ahead in the last days.

While the average Christian sleeps, the diabolic activity of the demonic continues to reap havoc among the work of God: *"While men slept his enemy came and sowed tares among the wheat…"* (Matthew 13:25). If Satan can hinder and sometimes stop the laborers of righteousness, he can stop the growth of the church, and yes, even hinder the growth of the Kingdom of God, even though he knows he will not win the war between darkness and light. We know that the Gates of Hell will not prevail, but there could be scores wounded in battle. Sowing tares among the wheat could mean sowing discord among the members of the congregation. Nothing destroys the Christian community faster than having its members bicker openly among themselves. Second, tares could mean tempting believers to sin. Of course there are always seeds of trials and problems the devil directs toward the Christian for the sole purpose to loose faith, or as Job's wife suggested for her husband, "Curse God and die."

We need to awaken; we need to cry aloud; we need to charge the very gates of hell with the willingness to reach into the flames and grab hold of that man, woman, child, or loved one and pull them to safety. We can do this with the assurance that Christ came seeking whosoever will called upon His name will be saved. Because Christ is with us, the brimstone of hell is unable to singe a single hair of the secure born-again believer. Remember the three Hebrew boys walked from the fiery furnace unscathed. Amen!

Sleeping During the Time of Prayer.

Too often, we are sleeping while our brothers and sisters in the faith need our support. When Christ walked the earth, He was very alone. As His ministry was about to end on earth, it was Satan's idea to kill Him or to cause so much mental pressure to come upon Him that Christ, abhorring the concept of becoming sin, might seek an escape by committing suicide before arriving on Calvary. The motion picture, *The Passion* captures this aspect in the opening scenes. The temptation was real: *take this cup from me* – maybe even *take this cross from me*. But it was the will of the Father, not the Son's that was followed. Jesus was obedient to the Father's purpose.

One would be amazed at the increased rate of suicide among Christians. (There are about 32,000 suicides committed in America annually. The national averages, including Christians, amounts to almost 20 people taking their own life for every 100,000 that make up the population.) Hundreds of believers, who should have everything to live for, have tossed life aside to take a less painful route, that of death. Of course Christians have the same anxieties and illnesses as anyone else, but only the Christian has the sure hope of everlasting life and a home in heaven. We need to be reminded that Christ walks with each believer. If God notices a sparrow's fall in the forest, how much more does He know about our own needs and battles? Likewise, I am sure the average person would be amazed at the emotional pressures placed upon men, women, and children in the ministry. The rate of ministers leaving the work due to emotional strain is staggering. Pastor Mark Driscoll of the Resurgence Research Group presented the Blackmon & Hart report on his blog. They (B & H) are strategists for the Clergy Assessment Career & Development. Their findings found that 12% of all ministers have suffered some level of depression during their time in the ministry. Their data also revealed that modern clergy (unlike the pastors of my Great-great Grandfather's day) have experienced (70%) major distress due to the demands placed upon them. Distress and depression in conjunction to family problems could be the underline element that caused 33% of American pastors to "call it quits." For one reason or another, 1,500 ministers leave the ministerial work every 30 days. (* For more information on this subject, the reader can log onto: www.theresurgence.com/mdblog_2006-05-24_death_by_ministry - 24k, or Google: Mark Driscoll.)

CHAPTER FOUR: SLEEPING SAINTS

Divorce among ministers and Christians in general is on the increase. I have known several such families who have experienced this kind of emotional anguish and setbacks. God has burdened my heart to reach out to the people setting in the pews that are under attack. There is a growing number of believers who have been cast aside by fellow Christians and forgotten by the church because of some besetting sin. It seems that we are the only organization that turns its back on its wounded especially when the sin falls into the immoral category. I wish we practiced more of what Jesus asked the Pharisees, *You who are without sin, cast the first stone*. The fallen Christian or pastor, at this time, needs someone to exhibit the love of Christ in which they preached more than ever. It seems one can be forgiven of every sin – even murder – but not immorality.

If all ministerial problems are becoming too heavy for pastors to endure, where are all the so-called prayer warriors? Where is the support of their church? Could it be that the "prayer warriors" and churchmen are sleeping while their brethren suffer? When have you last seen encouragement come when the darkness of Satan afflicted a fellow believer? How many Christians do you know who were willing to remain awake to pray all night for another believer? Can

MESSAGE FOUR: SLEEPING DURING PRAYER

you name a person who would be willing to visit the afflicted and read the scriptures to them? The average church hires a staff of ministers to make visits in the home and hospitals so the majority of the congregation can continue sleeping.

If we were honest, we would admit that we would rather let others lookout for themselves than to involve you and me. We do not want to hear about another person's problems; thus, we just shake our heads and turn away. Once or twice I asked for prayer due to sickness. The first response was, "Have you seen a doctor?" I did not ask for a doctor, I have that much common sense. I only asked for prayer for healing. Their response told me too few Christians truly believe that God still heals. There was a man whose infant son was badly burned in an accident. While he went through the earthly "hell" of seeing his own son along with 40 other children in the burn unit, some of his fellow Christians refused to support him because "they did not wish to become involved because he had too many problems." In my different ministries, there were always several ministers in the area that left their church for one reason or the other. I surmised that in most cases it was due to the lack of prayer in their individual congregations. I wondered myself, did I pray enough for them? Other times churches closed; I too can identify with this. In most cases the devil influenced certain ones from the congregation, usually those who have a strong personality, to sew discord among the brethren. In new churches, prayer, most often, is dependent upon only the pastor and his wife.

Where are the Aarons and Hurs today? Where are the brothers and sisters in Christ who would be willing to lift up our hands toward heaven (symbolically) in order for us pastors to be strengthened? You remember the story of Aaron and Hur (Exodus 17:10-12). Israel was in a battle. As long as Moses prayed with his arms lifted towards heaven, Israel prevailed, but when the man of God grew weary, (and we do) his arms fell to his side. When this occurred, Joshua began to loose the battle. Aaron and Hur quickly realized what was happening. The two men seated Moses on a rock and took positions on either side to support Moses' arms/hands toward heaven. There the men stood until the going down of the sun and the battle was won.

There are certain necessary ingredients for this type of victory. First, soldiers were needed on the battlefield to do the fighting. Secondly, a man of God was needed to give

MESSAGE FOUR: SLEEPING DURING PRAYER

divine guidance; finally, others were needed to support the man of God and the troops in the field. Every pastor needs prayer warriors. Ask yourself this question, Are you doing what you can for the cause of Christ? Are you doing what you can to support the local ministry as well as your home and community? Or are you slumbering in front of the television. Are you dedicated to enjoyment, easy living, and entertainment? Are you napping while Satan's pot boils in your town? Are you dozing while hundreds of fellow Christians are being actually killed by anxiety? Are you snoozing while missionaries are forced to return home for lack of financial support or because of the severity of their field's condition? Are you sleeping when others are in need of your help? Are you willing to stand with a minister of another faith in his hour of need?

Let us return to Christ's specific requests of His disciples to determine what is expected of us. Jesus asked Peter, James, and John to "tarry" (v.38), that is, set aside a time to pray, to study the Bible, to schedule a time to visit with one another.

He also asked the men to "watch with me." That is, be ready for danger; be on guard to resist the devil's temptations; to watch over your loved ones; to watch over those you have led to the Lord so that Satan does not sneak in and sow his tares of discouragement and false teaching on their doorstep. Watching is needed. Today, more than ever, we need to see where Satan will attack next and be prepared, "watchman what of the night" (Isaiah 11:11). Watching allows us time to get ready. Watching gives us strength to ward off Satan's attacks and lies. Finally, Christ asked His Apostles to pray. They were to remain awake and pray. Prayer is in itself worship and work, but they were too sleepy to ask for strength, guidance, or deliverance for themselves and others because of Satan's grip of sleep.

Satan already has a fast hold upon the lost. He will not surrender them without a struggle. The Devil many times only leaves its host in direst; that is, the demon will inflict as much pain as possible when he exists his victim, (Mark 9:26). If anyone should be demon possessed, and the demon leaves, we know from scripture and experience that he could return, (Luke 11:24-26). There is only one way to purge a man's soul from this process – get him saved. But you will never be able to accomplish this by indolent sleeping.

Are you sleeping? Are you in a stupor while drugs

destroy the lives of men and women around you? Are you sleeping while alcohol deadens the minds of men and youth alike, robbing them of reason and a slow death? Are you dozing while evil philosophies continue to infiltrate our schools (i.e., minds of the youth) through the media and apostate churches? Are you in dreamland while entire families drift apart, and the teachings of God and His truth continues to be relegated to the status of fables? WE DARE NOT SLEEP!! The consequences are too terrible to contemplate; they will affect all of us. Have you refused to develop programs and ministries that will provide a lifeboat for many in your community? Preaching has its place but so does walking with the individual – being a friend or just a neighbor to those willing to listen.

Sleeping While Danger Lurks in the Shadows to Devour

"Be not deceived," Jesus warns. Satan always attacks from an advantaged position. He is compared to a roaring lion in 1 Peter 5:8. He stalks consistently searching for that innocent or unsuspecting sheep. The night of Christ's trial, prior to his crucifixion, the whole city came out for Jesus with torches, swords and the temple guard. Worse! The religious leaders of the day were in that crowd to disavow any authority Jesus may have claimed. There is grave danger in all this, and it is upon us today! The present danger is to silence the preaching that saves men's souls. Satan's first work is to substitute the vitality of the gospel ministry and biblical preaching with a message of social humanitarianism (secularism) that can not rise above the devil's prime victim: man. Second, Satan's intent is to deceive the men and women of God, i.e., to trip them with compromises that will bring enough public embarrassment to force them from the ministry.

I have seen in my time a frontal attack upon churches; in fact, attacks have branched out to touch the very fiber of Christian belief. Memorials depicting the Ten Commandments have been removed by court order. Prayer has been denied in public places and on school campuses. Apostate churches and the courts have accepted perversion. One should see the writing on the wall of the rights and freedoms that was once enjoyed by all American citizens being surgically removed from the different communities. Christian schools are being closed because they do not conform to modern social theory. Thus, parochial schools are under unprecedented attack. Hitler said that if he were given the power to educate any nation's children, he would control that country in one or two generations. America's humanistic society wishes to control what each child learns void of parental influence from the time of birth onward. Dare we so surrender the next generation of believers because we are too lazy to rise from slumber?

My friend, it is time for serious praying; not generic praying or Mickey Mouse praying? We cannot afford to sleep any longer. The hour is coming when the believer will not be able to openly witness for his Lord. Judgment has already begun at the church and I see cruel, vicious, and heartless forces encircling our neighborhoods and state capitals daily.

Tarry, watch, and pray is the command. Remain busy in the Lord's work to avoid entering into temptation. Idle hands and minds do find mischief. We must work while we yet have time; while there is still a modicum of freedom to get the job done and while it is still called day. Darkness (demonic influence) is fast approaching. Are you saved? Have you been baptized? Are you actively serving in a church? We are not masters of time – physical death lies just a breath away.

Let us pray: *Dear Lord, please forgive me for not praying as I should have. I now realize that prayer, more than a form* *of worship, is in its simplest form a conversation between a son or daughter and his or her Father. What offspring would not want to talk to his parent; what Father would not want His offspring to converse with him. Forgive me and others of my Christian brethren in placing more emphasis on the more glorified and physical works of worship and not in humble prayer. Holy God, let me join the Apostles in requesting, "Lord teach us to pray." Dear Holy Spirit, guide us to the place of prayer. Give us the correct words to say and the correct ministry and people to pray for. Dear Jesus, take our meager requests and make intercession on our behalf to the Father. Allow the Spirit to work within us and around us. Send angels to assist humankind. Let prayer time become a joy; In Jesus' name. Amen!*

— MESSAGE FIVE —

SLEEPING WHILE THE LORD TARRIES HIS RETURN

Mathew 25:1-5: *Then shall the kingdom of heaven be likened unto ten virgins, which took their lamps, and went forth to meet the bridegroom. And five of them were wise, and five [were] foolish. They that [were] foolish took their lamps, and took no oil with them: But the wise took oil in their vessels with their lamps. While the bridegroom tarried, they all slumbered and slept.*

The first message in this five point series gives the reader an overall picture or characteristic of a sleeping Christian. The reader has learned that there was little difference in appearance between the carnal (sleeping) Christian and a lost person. The reader has learned that sleeping saints had a tendency to be unconcerned over their state of well being as well as the condition of a lost society. The sleeper is unable to even hear an alarm (if any is given) to alert the community of danger.

The second message dealt with congregations that had the appearance of sleeping during the preaching service. The letters to the seven churches, given in the Book of Revelation, were used to illustrate how much slumber was present when God was trying to awake the church to action.

The setting for the third message was upon the Mountain of Transfiguration. Peter, James, and John were sleeping when Jesus changed His appearance into His future glorified state. The Apostles missed the over-all discussion that transpired between Jesus, Moses, and Elijah. Sleeping saints are unable to discern what God may be trying to teach the church today via the preaching due to their slumbering attitude.

The forth message warns the church that the enemy easily attacks when congregations refuse to stay alert enough to pray for power and protection against the forces of Satan. While in the state of slumber, the Christian does

MESSAGE FIVE: SLEEPING WHILE THE LORD TARRIES HIS RETURN

not see the enemy positioning his ranks for an attack, nor is the sleeping saint alert enough to care about warning his community of the impending war that is about to commence. The finial message shows the return of the Savior for the church prior to unleashing the judicial twenty-one woes upon earth.

We are faced with the shameful fact that Christians are sleeping spiritually while their Christ is actively interceding on their behalf. *Who [is] he that condemneth? [It is] Christ that died, yea rather, that is risen again, who is even at the right hand of God, who also maketh intercession for us* (Romans 8:34). *Wherefore he is able also to save them to the uttermost that come unto God by him, seeing he ever liveth to make intercession for them* (Hebrews 7:25). There are many scriptures that inform the Christian that Juses is actively working for His children. First Timothy chapter two, verse five, shows Jesus working as mediator between God and man. First John chapter two, verse one goes one-step further to list the work of Jesus as a believer's advocate or attorney. Likewise, the believer has the Holy Spirit interceding for him as well as aiding in his prayer life, (Romans 8:26, 27).

Chapter Four: Sleeping Saints

The situation is at best anomalous, but it more accurately must be described as shameful! We ought not to be caught napping while Christ continues to plead our case before God the Father. Satan never sleeps; never stops trying to tempt us; and he never stops trying "to drag our names through the mud of sin before God." Paul warns us to *Awake to righteousness and sin not*, (1 Corinthians 15:34). In addition to this, Jesus warned future disciples that the enemy would sow tares (hindrances) among the wheat (Christians). Believers can not afford to slip into a spiritual slumber with such a persistent and powerful enemy on the loose.

Many Christians tend to relax once they are saved. However, no man poses a threat to the devil until he is saved. Too many Christians look upon receiving Christ as a long-term investment: a deferral of all responsibility and obedience to be cashed in at the last hour. Modern Christians look upon salvation as a hedge against the horrors of hell. They hope to accrue a heavenly claim while living for pleasure, money, and achievement. The aforementioned persons may not be true Christians; God only knows who belongs to the heavenly family.

MESSAGE FIVE: SLEEPING WHILE THE LORD TARRIES HIS RETURN

Sleeping While Others Drop Off Into Hell

In Proverbs 11:30, we read: *The fruit of the righteous is a tree of life and he that [wins] souls is wise.* God intended for Christians to be fruitful, bearing the fruit of saved souls. This is the very wisdom of God! It is how the saved pleases God, because God's overall plan is to redeem mankind from his lost state. Truly, we are saved to serve, not to sit and sleep. Be assured that if one sits and sleeps long enough, he will sour and be good for nothing.

Dr. Curtis Hutson, former pastor of the Forrest Hills Baptist Church of Decatur, Georgia, has often said, before going home to be with the Lord, "If the lost souls in this world would stand in a single file that line would circle the earth three times, and the line would grow twenty miles each day." He further testified, "If the present growth of population ceased or was frozen, it would take Christians at least until the year 3,000 A.D. to win the whole world, if they continued to evangelize at their present rate." He preached his statistics over thirty years ago. I often wonder what he would say about the present slumbering church that has exchanged worship for entertainment, true evangelism for excessive church activity, and conferences instead of spiritual revivals. The cry for repentance is not heard

CHAPTER FOUR: SLEEPING SAINTS

radiating from a sleeping congregations or pulpits.

Christ came to earth to lay down His life in order that man might be saved. Salvation is important to Him. While He was on earth, He ceased not to teach and preach the Gospel; likewise, He will not refuse anyone who comes unto Him. Saving/forgiving people was important enough for Jesus to have commissioned the twelve Apostles, the seventy disciples, and then all believers everywhere to tell the Good News. The Great Commission is given five times in scripture: once in each of the four Gospels and again in the Book of Acts. It was important and urgent enough to put Paul to the task of traveling great distances to witness and build churches in every city or settlement he visited. It is important enough to continue to call every man, woman, boy, and girl to the task of soul winning because the redeemed of the earth are few in number. (The so-called cults around the world are not slowing down; in fact, they are growing by leaps and bounds. The Mormon Church in America has more members than the Presbyterians and Episcopalians combine, according to the special 2003 edition of *U.S. News and World Report*.) Christians should presently be concerned with the staggering growth of Islam in the U.S. There are more than 1,200 Mosques in the United States, and they are 94% filled Friday during the time of prayer. It is unsure how many Muslims there are in America, but the latest estimate was 9 million. Because of America's open borders, most conservative Christians believe that number is steadily growing. In fact, Christendom should wake up to the fact that the Islam religion is the fastest growing religion in the nation toping out all known cults combined. The goal of Islam is to see their population grow to 50 million strong in America by the year 2030. Because of the media's spin and the liberal overtone found among the Hollywood crowd, Congress, and university campuses, very few American citizens realize that the Islamic doctrine is one of hate, not love or even toleration. If we are unable to convert the Arabic or Muslim population to Christianity, (which would be difficult, but not impossible) at least we should be busy trying to win others before Islam has a chance to sway that portion of the American population. According to Romans chapter one, we should all make note as Satan's darkness becomes thicker as time goes on; it will be more difficult to save the lost in the latter hours before the time of the Tribulation. More over, the U.N. has been trying for years to persuade Congress to pass a law forbidding any one, but especially Christians, from proselytizing a person away from his or her national or birth religion.

Hell is not an imaginary place! It was made for the

Chapter Four: Sleeping Saints

devil and his angels; furthermore, it will be the final ***"non-resting place"*** for all who rebel against God. As heaven was made for the believer to experience rest (Hebrews 4), hell was created for the devil and his angels and for the lost souls of man where there will be no such thing as rest (Matt**hew** 25:41). In fact, the souls of the damned will experience unrest for eternity. People end up in hell because they chose to follow the devil's easy road. Hell is like a scorpion, there is a poisonous sting at the end. Hell is a place without peace; a place of torment where sin's final bill is paid. To escape hell, one must be saved by/through Jesus Christ. The Messiah said, "I am the Way, the Truth, and the Life" – NO ONE PASSES INTO HEAVEN WITHOUT GOING BY HIM! (John 14:16) (My emphases – paraphrased). However, many could be like the Ethiopian eunuch when approached by Philip, when he asked, "Do you understand what you are reading? The eunuch answered, "How is it possible for me to do so unless someone explains it to me and guides me [in the right way]?" (Acts 8:30-31, Amplified). Were you to meet your own version of the Eunuch or the Philippian jailer, would you be awake enough to show him, his family, and friends the way leading to salvation? Or would you be content to sleep, ignoring their cry for help? If you or the church fail to witness, the lost, who may be your neighbor or member of your own family, will cry forever and ever, and ever in hell!

Sleeping During the Time of Harvest

The Gospel of Matthew gives us (20:1-9) an account about a man who went out to hire workers for the harvest. He went out to hire workers the first hour of the workday. He then went out to hire men the third hour also. The owner of the estate sent the foreman out to hire people the eleventh or the last hour of the day to help bring in the harvest. Workers were still standing idle in the evening. Friends, I believe in my heart that it is the eleventh hour before the Lord returns for His church. The harvest is not complete, so what is the reason so many of those who call themselves Christians still stand idol when the harvest is so plenteous and the labors are so few (Matthew 9:36-39). We should never fear the loss of wages. The Holy and unchanging God has promised all who labor for Him will receive an eternal reward, no matter which hour you went into the fields.

Nevertheless, we still find Christians behaving in a paradoxical manner. Christians believe, since they are now old, they either have too little time to do God's work, or they believe that their remaining hours should be spent upon personal matters. It is never time to retire from God's vineyard. If the Bible is correct in saying that our days are numbered, why tarry? Would it not be better to spend what time remains of life serving God in one's own eleventh hour? By this time, we should have the knowledge and experience and should not be quickly deterred or discouraged. Those in their golden years should at least be training others for the years ahead if the Lord decides to put off His return in order that one more soul might be saved.

Then there are Christians who stop working because the task is so great. They are looking at the vastness of the field and see few workers; they become disheartened and leave the work. Of course these saints forget that the harvest belongs to the Lord; it is the Lord's responsibility. We are unable to save anyone, but God can deliver whosoever He wills. It is He who sends forth laborers into the harvest. The church is not our own personal possession; rather, she belongs to God. He does all the saving and forgiving.

Moreover, there are those who are so deeply asleep spiritually that they either do not even see the harvest, or

MESSAGE FIVE: SLEEPING WHILE THE LORD TARRIES HIS RETURN

worse, they can not see the doom hanging over mankind. The sun is becoming warmer for that eventful Day of Judgment and hell has enlarged itself for the increase number of residents that are heading its way. We are becoming more like the disciples when they were near Jericho. They went into town in search of food rather than souls. They were concern over their physical need rather than the spiritual condition of the city. In contrast, the woman at the well left her work of gathering water to return to a town that had labeled her an outcast to tell them that she had met the Messiah. She not only tells of the good news, but also invites them to follow her back to the place where she left him sitting. What was the difference? The Samaritan woman believed who Jesus said He was. She was so full of joy and so awake to the fact that morning she was lost, but by the afternoon she had a new understanding from trusting the Master Himself for her salvation. She wanted to share the good news; she wanted the town to learn of the same hope she had. In short, it took a fallen woman who had been saved, whose eyes had been opened, to stand her town on its ear for two whole days. Lead someone to the Lord and that one will bring others to Christ (in your direction); but those who sleep can do nothing. *Say not there are yet four months and then come the harvest, behold I say unto you, life up*

Chapter Four: Sleeping Saints

your eyes [wake up!] and look on the fields for they are white already to harvest. (John 4:35). Solomon said in Proverbs 10:5: *...he that gathers in summer is a wise man, but he that sleeps in the harvest is a son that brings shame to the family,* (paraphrased).

We would not have half the people that God used to spread the Gospel in our pulpits or perhaps even as members of our churches. Peter cursed; Paul persecuted and imprisoned Christians; Thomas doubted; David danced and committed adultery; Moses had a temper; Elijah and Jonah wanted to commit suicide; Jeremiah preached for years without any converts; the Syrophoenician woman was of a different race, and the woman at the well was divorced. Many others had demons and several were prostitutes. Thank God He changes and recycles all who honestly come to Him. We should not view people in the 21st Century as second class Christians that have the same characteristics as those mentioned above, nor should we forbid them as unqualified laborers in the Kingdom of God.

Sleeping While Christ Prepares Heaven for Our Arrival

While Jesus is in heaven preparing a place for His beloved Bride, what are you doing while He tarries His

Message Five: Sleeping While The Lord Tarries His Return

return? (I have asked myself the same questions.) Have you added any wisdom or talent to Christ's Kingdom or are you simply accumulating possessions here on earth? Have you ever invited anyone to the Lord's wedding feast or were you content to printing wedding invitations for friends? Have you been awake enough to prepare for the next life or are you totally concerned with this life and have forgotten about the one that will be forever? For any one of us to believe that we will enter into eternity in this present physical form is life's most obscene delusion. No! Christ is preparing a place for all who have believed. He has made another body for the spiritual kingdom; He as reserved a place for each saved person at a table (Wedding Feast), He has even thought of and preserved a special wedding garment for all of us who have answered His invitation to be born again.

We have been fortunate in having been given time to repent of our laziness. God is longsuffering. The people of Noah's time were given 120 years to repent before the flood came. The people of Nineveh had 40 days to change their ways, which they did. The church in Thyatira was given a space of time to turn from her wicked ways. God does not take joy in disciplining or judging an individual or city or nation. But, I am afraid that our time to work is running short. The Trade Center tragedy, the western fires, southern floods, or droughts, city shootings, economic collapse, etc., are all merely the preliminaries pointing to the judgments that will come during the Tribulation. God is trying to awake this nation so she can return to the God she once knew and followed. From Paul's writing to the Church in Thessalonica, we learn that God is restraining, by way of the Holy Spirit, all evil that one day will be unleashed. Until then, He continues to prepare for our arrival.

Sleeping So Soundly That We Loose Our Reward

The parable found in Matthew 25:1-5 carries the account of the wise and foolish virgins. Most preachers of the word of God extol the wise virgins because they made themselves ready for the coming of the Bridegroom. They had oil (the Holy Spirit – the evidence of salvation) in their lamps, while the foolish virgins had no oil. Remember, "He that has not the Spirit has not Christ." However, allow me to point out some other factors in this parable that many have missed. Of the ten, all were virgins – both the foolish and the wise. They were alike in that respect. Both groups were waiting for the Bridegroom, i.e., the Lord Jesus Christ. All the virgins had lamps, i.e., souls. The problem is seen that only five had oil to burn for light. The real analogy that I wish to

MESSAGE FIVE: SLEEPING WHILE THE LORD TARRIES HIS RETURN

point out is this: while the Bridegroom delayed His coming (v.5), *all of the virgins slumbered and slept.* Although the wise virgins were ready to meet the Bridegroom, they were willing to sleep, and willing to loose additional awards. Consequently, they should have remained awake with the hope of winning their sisters to the Lord. They could have shared the location (gospel church) where to find the proper oil for their lamps before the Bridegroom's arrival.

In the same book and chapter we need to consider the parable of talents. One man, who received one talent, buried it instead of putting it to use. When the Lord called him to account for his talent, the man confessed that he merely buried the small prize. (Can anything given by the Lord be considered small or worthless?) The Lord labeled that man "wicked and slothful." What does this mean to us today? It most certainly means that our salvation is not the termination of our responsibilities toward God. On the contrary, life begins at salvation; we begin to grow in the Lord hopefully becoming more like Him each day. Life is a gift; therefore, once we are saved, we should be willing to use that life for the glory of God. Question: Would you be satisfied with having a child who laid in a lifelong coma? It would break your heart. God has a heart, too. Continue to sleep and you may well cause Him deep grief.

Yes, the night will come when no man will be able to work, but heaven's door is wide open. However, with the coming of the Bridegroom to take the souls of His saints, He shuts the door upon this age, (Matthew 25:10). This means that only those saved from Christ's resurrection until the Rapture will be called the Bride of Christ. There were people saved in the Old Testament economy and others that will be saved during the tribulation, but the 144,000 will be preaching the "Kingdom" as the prophets did in the years past. But, how about others; the Bible is clear there are those to whom the Lord will say, **"I know you not." I know you not!** Will your family, friends, city, or nation hear those words from the lips of Jesus? Will the statement, "I know you not," or "I never knew you," echo in your ears through eternity?

Wake up! Wake up to the fact that you have a predatory enemy sowing tares in your life. Wake up to the fact that you have the responsibility before God to be laboring for His Kingdom. Wake up to the fact that there is edifying preaching to be heard. Wake up to the fact that there is instruction in Godliness to be given. Wake up to the fact that God sent His Spirit to secure His children and to teach them of Himself. His assignment is to lead you along the way of life. You do not have to travel blind, in the dark, or by yourself. Wake up to the fact that souls can be saved, lives changed and delivered by your prayers – but more so by your labor. Wake up to the fact that the trumpet has not sounded and there is yet time to become involved. YES, WAKE UP! There is still room in our churches and still room at the Marriage Feast in Heaven. *Awake to righteousness, and sin not; for some have not the knowledge of God: I speak [this] to your shame* (I Corinthians 15:34,) *Awake thou that sleepest, and arise from the dead, and Christ shall give thee light* (Ephesians 5:14).

• • •

I pray that these messages have been and will continue to be a blessing to you. If the reader is a layman, you too need to be awake. Pastors, wake up and look at your ministry with a fresh vision. Call not a friend, but a respected church consultant to audit your work, and be willing to accept his counsel and consider any recommendations that may be offered.

To help make this message series memorable, the presenter could use Power Point to illustrate sleeping. Set up a cot in the foreyard, have pillows on the platform, or have the deacons wear sleeping caps. Have signs throughout the church depicting sleeping and the upcoming series. By all means, have your inner core leaders committed to pray for the services.

• • •

Notes:

US News Report, 2003

— CHAPTER FIVE: PART ONE —

Satisfying Man's Natural And Spiritual Needs For His Body And Soul

Part One: Text – I Thessalonians 5:23; Romans 8:5-12; Hebrews 4:12

Part Two: Text – John 12:20-21

— PART ONE —

Satisfying man's natural needs for his body

Introduction:

What is man? He is a trycodomy – one unit composed of

three parts. The divisions are: body, soul, and spirit. The Greek rendering is, *Soma, Psuke, and Pnuma* respectfully.

I Thessalonians 5:23: *And the very God of peace sanctify you wholly; and [I pray God] your whole spirit and soul and body be preserved blameless unto the coming of our Lord Jesus Christ.*

Note how many times the terms flesh and spirit are used in the following text.

Romans 8:5-12: *For they that are after the flesh do mind the things of the flesh; but they that are after the Spirit the things of the Spirit. For to be carnally minded [is] death; but to be spiritually minded [is] life and peace. Because the carnal mind [is] enmity against God: for it is not subject to the law of God, neither indeed can be. So then they that are in the flesh cannot please God. But ye are not in the flesh, but in the Spirit, if so be that the Spirit of God dwell in you. Now if any man have not the Spirit of Christ, he is none of his.*

To understand the different parts that make up man, one must observe the eternal characteristics of God who originally designed the human race. To answer the primary inquiry we need not search for a better resource than the Word of God. The reader should deduct, from the above texts, that we have a singular God with three personages. The doctrine of the Trinity (God the Father, God the Son, and God the Spirit) is laced throughout all scripture, but especially here. It says that the Spirit of God indwells the believer, and then the writer tells us that the Spirit of Christ lives in the believer. The Greek word for God is rendered as a singular noun *Theos*, but is displayed as being plural because of the plural verb. Furthermore, the Spirit of the Theos/God seems to be the same as the Spirit of Christ (one Spirit living in man). The double reference pictures a trycodomy if the Holy Spirit is considered living also in man. The verse further tells the reader, if mankind (male and female) does not have God's Spirit, he or she does not belong to God. Therefore, the person absent of the Living Spirit of God is not saved or born again.

The next text refers again to the trycodomy of human race.

Hebrews 4:12: *For the word of God [is] quick, and powerful, and sharper than any two-edged sword, piercing even to the dividing asunder of soul and spirit, and of the* *joints and marrow, and [is] a discerner of the thoughts and intents of the heart.*

The soul seems to be separate from the life source of the Spirit (*pnuma*) and the heart (psyche) of man. The joints and marrow speak of the body or flesh of a person. Therefore, each individual person is composed of a body, a soul, and a spirit.

The reader should immediately be aware there is a separation between the soul and spirit. The two different entities are then seen separate from the flesh signified by the "joints and marrow." The final thought of the text speaks of segments belonging to the soul, which is made up of the emotion, mind, and will. The "living" word of God, when spoken, has power to convict an individual of right and wrong by discerning (weighing the evidence) of the mind (thoughts) and the will (intents of the heart) clearly reveals man's further divisions. A closer examination or exegesis will reveal the meaning for the divisions of the soul as stated above. The discerner (*krilikos*), the Living Word of God, judges the mind of man as he reads the Scripture as to his thought life. Man's intent (*ennoia*) is the action he will take based upon his thoughts or the truth found in the Word. All

PART ONE: SATISFYING MAN'S NATURAL NEEDS FOR HIS BODY

this is said to prove humankind is more than mere flesh and blood. One could say the complexities of man seem to show he must have been patterned on purpose after the DNA of his Creator.

Another proof text that speaks of God's personages is found in the Great Commission: *Go ye therefore, and teach all nations, baptizing them in the name of the Father, and of the Son, and of the Holy Ghost* (Matthew 28:19). The baptismal command was given by Jesus Christ, Himself. Hence, if God is a trinity and God created man in His image, it seems rational to conclude that the human race would be similar to its Creator. (This is very important because several doctrines are substantiated in these verses.) Furthermore, by Apostle John saying, "God is Spirit," man too must have a spiritual nature. The spiritual nature of humans was fashioned in the "psuke" or soul. God gave man a body made from the earth and a soul patterned after heaven. Jesus, on the other hand, was made in the "likeness of man" having a body of flesh while retaining the Spirituality of Deity. In the end, those who believe in God and Christ will always have a spiritual body to house the soul, (2 Corinthians 5:1-3). Most scholars believe the Christian will have the same type of body as the resurrected body of Jesus Christ, (John 20:19-29).

Chapter Five: Satisfying Man's Natural And Spiritual Needs For His Body And Soul

There could be confusion in the words "made in the image of God after his likeness." I personally teach that the human race has the same characteristics as God the Father, i.e., eternal existence. The only difference being is that God has always been; whereas, humanity had a beginning. God will never cease to be; likewise, neither will man once he becomes a living organism. The only problem a person has is determining where he or she will continue to exist, in heaven with the Father and Christ or in hell with Satan. There is no reference given in scripture that speaks of man's annihilation like some beliefs proclaim.

One other thought on the subject that has been put aside until now that points to the trinity of God is the same verse that tells the reader man was created. *And God said, Let us make man in our image, after our likeness: and let them have dominion over the fish of the sea, and over the fowl of the air, and over the cattle, and over all the earth, and over every creeping thing that creepeth upon the earth. So God created man in his [own] image, in the image of God created he him; male and female created he them* (Genesis 1:26-27). The two possessive pronouns in the text, "us and our," should alert the reader to the possible existence of a single God.

There are scores of books and magazines on the

PART ONE: SATISFYING MAN'S NATURAL NEEDS FOR HIS BODY

market that speak of man having a mind, a body, and a spirit. Most of the references come from the New Age camp. They emphasize the spiritual but one should be careful when reading from these sources. The New Age "spiritual" is not the same as the "biblical spiritual." Man has a body or flesh that incorporates all the organs that sustain life. He also has a soul with three divisions: the emotion, the mind, and the will. The soul is the real person (the real you). It is the soul that is eternal. Because some scripture equates the spirit and soul as one, there could be some confusion. The reader needs to keep the scripture in context to determine which is which. Please remember that the soul is also spiritual in nature. (The difference between the spirit and the soul of man will be clarified later.) In reality it is the soul of man over which God and the devil are battling.

From man's birth Satan has been trying to shape the soul of man into his image. He uses temptations of the world and of the flesh including the man's fallen nature to work toward this end. On the other hand, from the rebirth of a believer, the Holy Spirit is trying to shape the soul of man into the image of Christ, (Romans 8:29; 1 Corinthians 11:7; Colossians 3:10). Consequently, the rebirth does not deter Satan from his objective (plan B) of trying to sidetrack

God's people from living successful lives. He can not prevent a person from being saved, but he can hinder the born again person from totally following God. This weakens heaven's objective. Satan may not be able to touch man's person, but if he can destroy man's character and testimony, like he tried to do with Job, Satan will make the Christian non-affective in laboring for the Kingdom of God.

The spiritual side of the individual has two sections that give life. One section gives life to the *soma* (body) in order for man to function. The second section gives life to the soul. The body and the soul are inter-related but not the same. For this reason the soul and the flesh are **not** one and the same. Re-emphasis is made because some faiths practice the unbiblical doctrine of "soul sleep." The Mormons and Jehovah Witness along with the Seventh Day Adventist teach that man's body lays in the grave asleep until the time of the rapture. It is a serious misinterpretation because it robs the believer of a proportional victory in Christ. The Savior told the Pharisees that Jehovah was the God of the living – not the dead.

Clearly, the Gospels show Christ's body lying in the tomb. It is learned from the Apostle Peter that Jesus (in spirit

PART ONE: SATISFYING MAN'S NATURAL NEEDS FOR HIS BODY

form) descended into Paradise in order to preach to the Old Testament Saints. It is Paradise and not the place of torment because of what Christ told the thief on the cross: *Today you will be with me in Paradise.* This further shows that Jesus did not continue to suffer in hell for man's sin with the rich man of Luke Chapter 16. Before He died, Jesus said, "It is finished." God the Father was satisfied with the sacrifice of His dear Son on the cross. It would not be continued beyond the grave. Moreover, man's emotions and memory will remain in tact after death (seen also in Luke 16). Whatever one does or fails to do on earth will be remembered in the next life. Memories are part of the soul and mind.

Since the fall of Adam, the power that gave life to the soul was taken; *the spark* went out or left the soul due to sin. This is called the "lost condition" that was brought about when Adam ate of the Tree of Knowledge of good and evil contrary to God's instruction not too. Thus, Adam fell from grace, and in his fall became a sinner; this condition was past on to all of his descendents, (Romans 5:12). The second side (See graphics below.) retains the spark of life in order to keep the flesh alive. Mankind can be alive physically, but dead spiritually. This is the reason Jesus pointed out the need for the rebirth to Nicodemus (John

Chapter 3). Paul revealed, whoever does not have the Spirit of God does not have life and will not see life because he does not belong to God (Rom. 8:5-12).

PART ONE: SATISFYING MAN'S NATURAL NEEDS FOR HIS BODY

THE TRYCODOMY OF MAN
— FIGURE 1 —

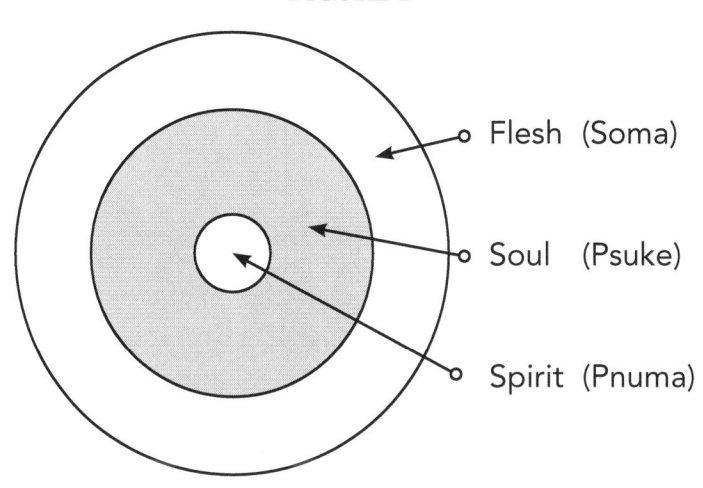

- Flesh (Soma)
- Soul (Psuke)
- Spirit (Pnuma)

GOD CREATED MAN WITHOUT SIN
— FIGURE 2 —

- Body
- Emotion / Mind / Will
- SOUL
- Spirit of Life for the Soul
- Spirit of Life for the Flesh

SLEEPING SAINTS 193

CHAPTER FIVE: SATISFYING MAN'S NATURAL AND SPIRITUAL NEEDS
FOR HIS BODY AND SOUL

THE FALL OF MAN

The soul died immediately due to sin –overtime
the flesh will likewise perish.

— FIGURE 3 —

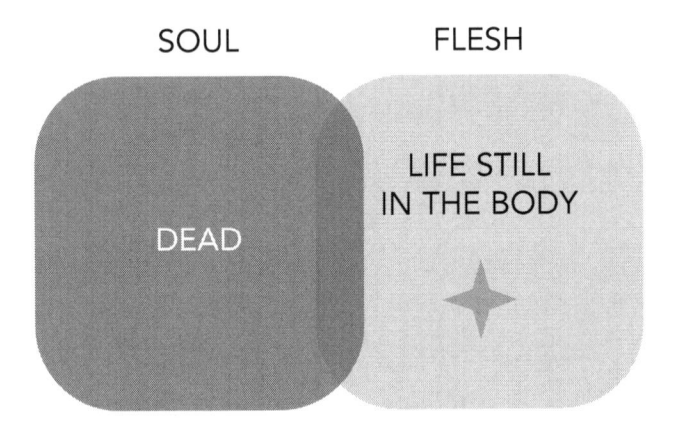

SOUL — FLESH

DEAD

LIFE STILL IN THE BODY

AT SALVATION MAN BEGINS TO LIVE AGAIN SPIRITUALLY

— FIGURE 4 —

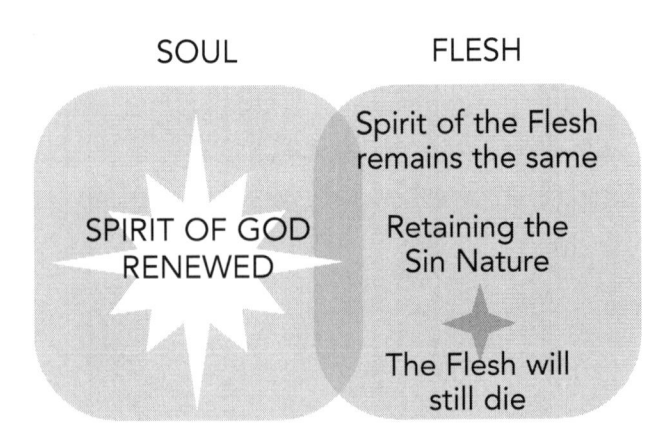

SOUL — FLESH

SPIRIT OF GOD RENEWED

Spirit of the Flesh remains the same

Retaining the Sin Nature

The Flesh will still die

194 SLEEPING SAINTS

PART ONE: SATISFYING MAN'S NATURAL NEEDS FOR HIS BODY

Mankind on a whole needs some important elements for each of his three parts.

The Body
The first element man needs to sustain life is **air** to breathe.

Meteorology is the study of the atmosphere that surrounds the planet. The atmosphere is composed of a number of different gases: nitrogen makes up 78% of the air we breath; oxygen is presently at 21%. Our lungs are made up of more than 700 million air sacks known as alveolus that collects air before it is deposited into the blood. The blood then distributes the collected oxygen to every cell in the body. (Creational scientists believe, due to recent discoveries of fossilize organic matter, oxygen content upon the earth was at a greater volume before the cataclysmic flood; earth has been loosing traceable amounts of oxygen ever since. The continual decrease of oxygen, of late, is believed responsible for the continuing development of incurable diseases.) The air surrounding earth is composed of argon, carbon dioxide, helium, methane, krypton, hydrogen, and ozone. These gases mixes is with water vapor and extends hundreds of miles into space and serves as a buffer zone against radiation and meteors that bombard the planet on a daily basis. The atmosphere makes earth different from the other eight worlds in this solar system.

After five minutes without air to breathe, man begins to develop problems maintaining consciousness. Without oxygen in the blood, the brain and other vital organs will suffer damage. God developed a balanced system. On one side man exhales carbon dioxide (CO_2) which is poisonous to him, but green vegetation is made to absorb carbon dioxide gases. Plant life gives oxygen in exchange for the carbon dioxide. Scientists are concerned over the destruction of vast acres of forests around the world, but particularly the Rain Forest in South America. Earth was created with an abundance supply of oxygen. On the other hand, if we ever were able to visit another planet, the number one payload aboard would be a supply of oxygen and water. No planet in our solar system supports an adequate water supply that will allow sufficient plant life to produce enough oxygen to maintain life.

The second important element man needs to survive is **water**.

We can live only a few days without this substance. As stated above, this too makes earth different from other

PART ONE: SATISFYING MAN'S NATURAL NEEDS FOR HIS BODY

planets since 70% of the earth's surface is covered with water. Man appears to be walking water bags because his red blood cells constitute 60% water and his blood plasma is 92% water. Man's muscle tissue is almost 80% water. Nutritionists tell us to drink eight glasses of water a day. If each glass holds eight ounces, the daily water intake for an individual should be 64 ounces. This is important because water is another deterrent to disease because it tends to flush pollutants from the body.

Water is unique in itself. It serves man internally and externally. It not only sustains life for the body; it also servers as a solvent. Mankind cleanses himself and his tools with water. This element can be found in three forms upon earth: liquid (water), solid (ice), and vapor (steam). Therefore, man needs air and water to survive.

The third important element man needs to sustain the flesh is **food**.

Whereas man can only survive a few minutes without air, a few days without water; he can live only a few weeks without food. Food is used to build and/or repair tissues as well as a fuel to supply energy. This substance is found in proteins, carbohydrates and fats. Verse 12 of

CHAPTER FIVE: SATISFYING MAN'S NATURAL AND SPIRITUAL NEEDS FOR HIS BODY AND SOUL

Genesis chapter one seems to imply that man was a vegetarian in the beginning, *And the earth brought forth grass, [and] herb yielding seed after his kind, and the tree yielding fruit, whose seed [was] in itself, after his kind.* After the flood, man was permitted to add certain meats (flesh of animals) to his diet. Currently, the human race is producing enough pollution in the earth to jeopardize the longevity of these life-giving substances. God, on the other hand, gave the earth the ability to cleanse itself of many of the harmful contaminates that would annihilate all life.

The fourth item man needs to sustain the body is **sleep**.

The Bible calls this aspect *rest*. God divided the light from the darkness. The light he called day and the darkness he called night. Man was made for the light. Matter of fact, diverse things will happen to humans if he is exposed to long periods of darkness. The Bible further divides the twenty-four hour day into three eight-hour shifts.

One shift is for sleep or state of rest. In this state the physiological function of the body slows. Man breathes less often and the heart beats less times because less energy is required. There are several cycles of sleep man experiences during this period. First, there is the S-cycle, which makes up three-fourths of the period of sleep. The second period is called the D-cycle. It is known as the paradoxical deep sleep period – paradoxical because the nervous system is very active. It is also known as REM sleep or the dream stage. Without this period man will become hallucinogenic or disoriented in a few days (Harris & Levey).

Man has developed food disorders as well as disorders of sleep, better known as sleep deprivation. This is when the REM period is interrupted. Jet lag is when man's circadian cycle (internal clock) becomes confused to the actual time of day. Many people experience this time variation the first few weeks after day light saving time is instituted or when a person crosses several time lines in a short period (Harris and Levey, p. 2537).

During sleep the mind rests; this allows a more calm stage of activity to catalog the day's experiences. In some conditions the body may put itself to sleep on purpose in order to make repairs. Since God created a balanced universe, day and night make up weeks and years that give man time to accomplish what is required to live on earth. The Bible tells us that there is a time to die, to kill, to heal, to break down, to build up, to weep, to laugh, to mourn, to

CHAPTER FIVE: SATISFYING MAN'S NATURAL AND SPIRITUAL NEEDS
FOR HIS BODY AND SOUL

dance, etc. (Ecclesiastes 3:1-8). All requirements or needs to sustain life must be balanced. Too much air, water, food, or sleep is equally harmful to man as is too little.

Humanity needs three additional items to fulfill a balanced and productive life. The latter three deal within the hidden element of man's make-up, his psyche or his emotional side.

Man's Emotions

This part of humanity is not seen by the naked eye, but still exists nonetheless. This element is found in both the physical and spiritual aspect of man, which will be presented in more detail in part two seen below.

A number of scholars have discounted the emotional division of man unimportant because they believe, if any emotional problem develops, it is merely in a person's mind and should not to be considered part of reality. To the contrary, David G. Benner's book, *Healing Emotional Wounds* (1990), said that the emotional side of man is indeed real and it further "operates according to its own laws." He went on to point out:

"Just because the emotions do not follow the laws of logic, does not mean they are less real. Unseen fears or phobias are so real to some people that it can result in their death. For example, a person who suffers from claustrophobia could literally suffocate in an elevator. The thought could be imaginary but the person will be dead nonetheless because the brain perceived the walls of the elevator closing in like a tomb; thus, shutting out the air."

Mankind was not made to live alone. He needs people around him. **Friendship**, therefore, is a relationship characterized by the enjoyment of each other's company, acceptance, respect, and a willingness to assist one another. This brings understanding and an opportunity to share experiences, feelings, spontaneity, trust, and a sense of belonging (John Collins, *Christian Counseling*, 1988, p. 370).

Collins found in the early years of the 20th Century according to Dr. Wm. Hocking, professor of philosophy at Harvard University, that man needed friends or human companions in order to live a balance and productive life. He further believed that "ready made" friends were hard to find, if not impossible. True friendship must be developed. This

Chapter Five: Satisfying Man's Natural And Spiritual Needs For His Body And Soul

development falls upon the person who desires a mature relationship. Such a person must first show himself friendly. His friendliness will attract another person who may be equally searching for the same relationship. It must be pointed out any bonding in the beginning does not mandate a intimate love affair that will evolve into marriage. Man needs male friends the same as a woman needs to have female friends.

Sociologists classify the human race as being made up of singles, married, family, groups, communities, cities, and societies. The scientists (Harris & Levey) have done extensive studies on each of the listed divisions. In the list there are people who are lonely. The number of lonely people grows daily. It has been said a man is rich if he has five people he could call a friend. The millions of lonely people are a by-product of modern society. The paradox states a person can be lonely in a crowd. We live in a society where one person does not know the name of his neighbor. If a problem arose, the average person would not have a close friend to call. A great need for any individual is to have a friend.

Part of the spiritual aspect of humanity that bridges the body and soul is known as the *"will."* Working in this area there is the element known as **motivation** – "the will to do." Ambition and enthusiasm are two words that are used in conjunction pertaining to a human's emotional need. The stimulus to achieve enough motivation to get out of bed and go to work may be that work enables one to pay his or her bills. Other motivators could be love or the possibility that the individual likes what he or she does.

According to psychologist, Wyne Dryer, having a sense of purpose in one's life is the most important element of becoming fully functioning, (*The Sky's the Limit*, 1990). Purpose is the cause of a commitment list. If a person is void of this element that makes a person's worth seem non-beneficial, he will feel empty and unfulfilled. Low self-worth will bring on frustration, anxiety, and depression. The self-preconceived attitudes come from within. The average person knows the truth. He or she can make the flesh lie or deny what is true, but in the end what is hidden will be manifested openly. Sooner or later the lie will lead to a variety of illnesses that will resurface in some area of the body.

On the other hand, a number of people will never try to accomplish success in life for a number of reasons. For some, the endeavor will seem too difficult and they will quit. Others will loose their vision of a life's goal; consequently

CHAPTER FIVE: SATISFYING MAN'S NATURAL AND SPIRITUAL NEEDS
FOR HIS BODY AND SOUL

they will not review the original plan that caused them to initiate the challenge in the first place. Other times, a person will remain lost in a dream stage. Fantasizing remains in the mind until the unseen facts are replaced into action. Dreams must be written, organized, and steps devised for them to become a reality. Taking time to devise a plan of action is a good investment. In contrast there are scores of people who not only have a deep desire to succeed in life, they will continue feeding their desire with needed information to help over come any unforeseen set backs. For example, a million-dollar enterprise is writing self-help and motivational books for the seekers and doers. Resources are abundant. A person can make a substantial income by coaching people who want to succeed or wish to feel life is worth living. It is alarming to learn a great number of the present-day youth have no real ambition. Thousands of people seem to live to party, and the parties are growing beyond the weekends.

The third emotion man needs to fulfill is **love**. Most all people need to love someone as well as for someone to love them. This is a learned process. There must be a realization that there are three ways to express love: by word, by attitude, and – action and by sacramental action (W.L. Carrington, MD, *Psychology, Religion, and Human Need*, 1957).

PART ONE: SATISFYING MAN'S NATURAL NEEDS FOR HIS BODY

There should be no presupposition; we need to be told (and we need to hear) over and over that another person loves us. This way we know we are not alone in the world. The learning process comes into being when we learn how to express this emotion in words and action well pleasing toward another. The complexity of this human emotion is exhibited when love reaches maturity. Many times this level of love becomes too deep for words or actions. This is when love crosses into the spiritual realm; when two people have an unspoken understanding at the same time.

As air, water, food, and rest mandates balance, the emotion of love demands restraint especially when the social and cultural environment is considered. If the social and cultural factors become unbalanced or distorted, this emotion becomes abnormal to the individual exercising the emotion as well as to others around him.

We all need to be loved by someone and be able to give our love to another. Scientists have studied love in animal psychology to better understand love between humans. A story was once told about a group of scientists adopting a dog from the pound. They took excellent care of

Chapter Five: Satisfying Man's Natural And Spiritual Needs For His Body And Soul

it, petting it, feeding it, talking to the dog, and playing with the dog; thus, they treated it as a family pet although the setting was in a laboratory. They took a sample of bone marrow from the dog and found it to be pink, which revealed that the dog was producing good blood cells. The wound from surgery healed quickly. Afterwards, the scientists began ignoring the dog. They did not mistreat it, but withdrew all human contact from the animal. The dog soon withdrew itself of all sights and sounds of the lab. It retreated to sleeping under a desk the greater part of the day. Another sample of bone marrow was taken. This time, it was almost white which suggested it was not producing an adequate supply of red blood cells. The second wound took 3 to 4 weeks longer to heal than previously. In the third month, the scientists once more began to respond more positively toward the dog as a pet. Two months were allowed to past before another sample of bone marrow was taken. The third sample of bone marrow was pink again. From this evidence science concluded that love must play an important part in the health of an individual. It also verified that one's emotional state can and will affect the physiological health of a living emotional organism.

— CHAPTER FIVE: PART TWO —

SATISFYING MAN'S NATURAL AND SPIRITUAL NEEDS FOR HIS BODY AND SOUL

— PART TWO —
Satisfying man's spiritual needs for his soul

Text: John 12:20-21: *And there were certain Greeks among them that came up to worship at the feast: The same came therefore to Philip, which was of Bethsaida of Galilee, and desired him, saying,* Sir, ***we would see Jesus****.* (My emphasis.)

Introduction:

The reader has learned that mankind requires oxygen, water,

food, and sleep in order to function properly. Emotionally, he requires three additional items: friends, ambition, and love in order to live a balanced existence. Since the soul is considered an entity in itself, the reader will learn that the soul (*psuke*) requires the same seven necessities as the body and psyche. (Let us not forget that there is a crossover or a "meshing" of the body and soul so the two are interwoven as stated in the Part One.) In this gray area we find the mind and the will. Without this area in the brain, the body would not function properly.

As stated before, God the Father has certain characteristics and works that only He will do; likewise, the characteristics and work of the Son differs from the Father. The Holy Spirit has His own characteristics and works to accomplish; yet, there remains a single entity working together as Creator, Savior, and Teacher. The proof of this hypothesis is found in the following text: *Now there are diversities of gifts, but the same Spirit. And there are differences of administrations, but the same Lord. And there are diversities of operations, but it is the same God, which worketh all in all* (I Corinthians 12:4-6). Paul seemingly substantiates the premise of the Trinity further in his letter to the Ephesians: *[There is] one body, and one Spirit, even as ye are called in one hope of your calling; One Lord, one faith, one baptism, One God and Father of all, who [is] above all, and through all, and in you all* (Ephesians 4:4-6). The Apostle John also writes, *For there are three that bear record in heaven, the Father, the Word, and the Holy Ghost: and these three are one* (1 John 5:7). The preceding verse seems to show there are three personalities in the Godhead. In "Part One" I submitted that if God is trinity, it would be reasonable for Him to create man with the same characteristics as Himself; thus, the human race was created having a body, soul, and spirit.

According to a number of theologians, the soul of man is considered the highest or most important part of man. Thiessen wrote in his *Introductory Lectures in Systematic Theology* (1949) that the soul is considered the conscience of man, which is also immortal because of its Devine origin, *And the LORD God formed man [of] the dust of the ground, and breathed into his nostrils the breath of life; and man became a living soul* (Genesis 2:7). When God gave the spark of life, Adam began to live physically and spiritually. "Becoming a living soul" implies man is more soul or spirit than he is flesh. God identified man as a soul, not a body. Therefore, a real person is depicted as a soul. Scripture also states that the body is the "house" where the soul resides. In the end or for eternity, the redeemed will be given a glorified body to house the soul, "not made by hands... [that] we shall not be found naked." (2 Corinthians 5:1-3)

Therefore, mankind was created in the image of God; meaning, although humans had a beginning, they will not cease to exist. Accordingly, the human race was created in God's image after His likeness, placed upon earth to grow and mature, and to remain in full fellowship with his creator (See Figs. 2 and 5). When sin entered man's environment [Fig. 6]; he fell; thus, he was separated from fellowshipping with God. Humanity, due to Adam's sin, came into the world lost. When this occurred, all of mankind died spiritually. The section of the spirit that gave life to the soul went dark (Fig. 3). Consequently, under God's direction all of Adam's future offspring were lost or spiritually dead. *Wherefore, as by one man sin entered into the world, and death by sin; and so death passed upon all men, for that all have sinned:* (Romans 5:12). Adam's *lostness* became part of his DNA that was past on to his descendents like you and me. But God so loved His creation (John. 3:16), that He made it possible for man to live again or to be born again (John 3:3-7) (Fig. 7). Sin can not come into the presence of Holiness;

therefore, God devised a plan to redeem the human race back to Himself through Christ.

CHAPTER FIVE: SATISFYING MAN'S NATURAL AND SPIRITUAL NEEDS FOR HIS BODY AND SOUL

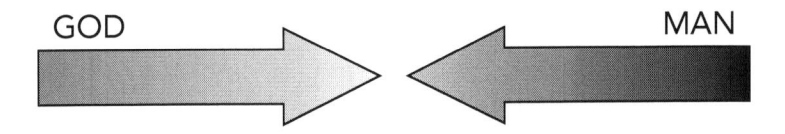

Genesis 1:26-27   Adam without sin had fellowship with God and God with man.

— **FIGURE 5** —

Genesis 3: 6-7   Sin separated God from man and man from God. Man had to turn from God to commit sin and God had to turn from man because of sin.

— **FIGURE 6** —

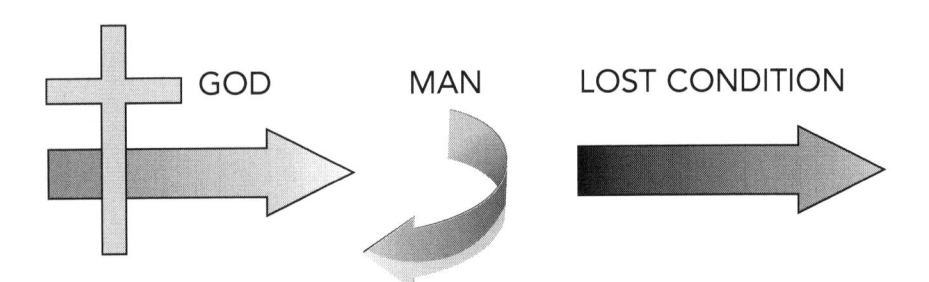

Salvation is available to all of humanity, "for whosoever will..." (John 3:16)
Ephesians 2:8, 9: (For by grace are we saved, through faith... it is a gift of God.)

— **FIGURE 7** —

Christ stands at the door of man's heart and knocks with the desire to come unto him. The possibility of being reconcile back to God can cancel all lost fellowship with God. Man was given the right/ability to make his own decision – to accept the free gift of salvation or to reject it. To reject God's graceful act would mean eternal death for the individual. The black arrow (Fig. 7) depicts man's rejection of the grace of God; thus, the non-repentant person will experience a spiritual death that will ultimately result in the eternal second death. Because of the cross of Jesus, man can either turn to God, "whosoever will," or he can continue down life's road and remain in his lost condition until his death. The Holy Spirit is the One who woos the lost person back toward God. Without the involvement of the Holy Spirit, mankind would not know of God's love, grace, and waiting forgiveness.

Please allow me to point out that Scripture, if taken literally, does not teach a "limited atonement." God so loved the world that Christ died for all. Scripture also teaches that salvation is free. Man can not work for it or do anything in order to obtain the rebirth. Paul stressed in his letter to the Galatians that salvation did not come by keeping the law, and his letter to the church at Ephesus presented salvation was a gift. If these two texts are true, and I believe they are, then Scripture does not teach a believer can loose his salvation or that he has to work in order to keep it.

Let me use the properties of a ballpoint pen to further illustrate the security of the believer. The slender reservoir that holds the ink represents the believer's soul. The ink becomes the indwelling Holy Spirit. The Holy Spirit is in the soul, which is part the body. At the same time, He flows out into the world (from the believer) to be a blessing to others. But the non-ending supply of God's Power remains present within (Romans 8: 3, 11; John 14:17, 23). As the pen's housing incases the tube of ink to protect it from outside forces, Jesus incases our soul that carries the chamber where the Holy Spirit resides to protect the soul, *"...they shall never parish, neither shall any man pluck them out of my hand,"* (John 10:28). When I place my hand around the fuselage of the pen, I represent God the Father, *"My Father...is greater than all and no man is able to pluck them out of my Father's hand,"* (v. 29). For someone to rob the supply of ink, the person must break my grip on the pen and then break the casing of the pen before coming in contact with the tube that holds the ink. The analogy is: before a believer can lose his salvation, some force must be able to break the Father's grip, the Son's grip, and then go through the protective force field that has been placed around the soul by the Holy Spirit (Ephesians 4:30) before any contact can be made with the flowing Spirit of God. Then the ink (Spirit) must be totally rinsed from the soul in order to place man in a new lost condition. Scripture says that the believer has "eternal life." One cannot lose something that is eternal. For a saved individual to become lost would mean a "second fall." The person would have to be born again a second time or as often as one finds himself in the lost condition. Thankfully, the Scripture clearly teaches contrary to this opinion.

Man needs the following in order to survive: air, water, food, sleep, friends, ambition, and love. The soul requires the same seven items for its survival. Where does he find the spiritual seven? One place comes to mind – the person, Jesus Christ. Moreover, man does not have to seek after these elements. Since an individual has asked for salvation, all seven ingredients are freely provided. The individual only has to freely accept the seven for them to mean something in his life.

As the men in the text were seeking Jesus, we also

should seek Jesus for the things of the soul and learn what benefits come with being born again or saved.

We Would See Jesus for Air

When God the Father breathed (*ruach*) into Adam, man began to live or began to be alive. The Father brought both the spark of life and the breath of life, e.g., a doctor uses a fibrillator (spark) to "jump start" the heart that has stopped beating. To sustain life oxygen/wind is forced (*naphach*) into the lungs to promote breathing. Similarly, when the rebirth of salvation is considered, Jesus applies the spark to the soul and breathes in fresh wind: *And when he had said this, he breathed on [them], and [said] unto them, Receive ye the Holy Ghost* (John 20:22). Jesus sends the Holy Spirit into the believer; hence, He is the spark and breath that returns life to the soul (Fig. 4). The Apostle John said, "in Him [Jesus] is life." Jesus told Mary and Martha in (John 11:25), that He was *"the resurrection and the life. He that believes though he was dead, yet shall he live."* Lazarus is a type of the lost or the spiritual dead who is made alive a second time. When Jesus breathed (*emphuso*) on the Apostles a gentle wind was used. In contrast, Ezekiel was commanded to preach (Chapter 37) to the four winds (*anemos*) commanding them to blow on all corpses that were laid out on the valley floor. When the wind gave breath to the men, they stood up a strong living army.

Another mighty wind (*pnoe*) was used on the Day of Pentecost (Acts 2:2). When the Holy Spirit came as a great wind, it filled the upper room; and in so doing, the Spirit gave power and boldness to all that were gathered in prayer. The cloven tongues of fire are representative to the spark that is needed to bring life (jump start) to man's soul.

Therefore, in order to be made spiritually alive, we need to see Jesus. By accepting, through faith, His work on the cross, He forgives our sins and applies the blood to cleanse the soul from the stain of sin. The cleansing, according to most biblical scholars, prepares the area that will receive the Holy Spirit who regenerates the total soul or heart of man. The mind, emotion, and will are included in the process. The soul of man is sealed by the same Spirit until the day or redemption, (Ephesians 4:30). Salvation or the event where the lost/dead is made alive again happens so instantaneous that he cannot measure it in time. I have only broken down the event into steps in order that we may understand the process it took in order for humanity to understand what is meant by being born again.

Chapter Five: Satisfying Man's Natural And Spiritual Needs For His Body And Soul

We understand that Jehovah is the only Deity that is to be worshipped, (Exodus 20:3). We can begin to understand the Trinity of God more fully by accepting the different roles that each person of the Godhead does. It appears the Holy Spirit does much of the work, but the believer must equally realize that by accepting Jesus, he is accepting the Godhead. For example, Romans 8:9-10 states: *,,, if so be that the Spirit of God dwell in you. Now if any man have not the Spirit of Christ, he is none of his. And if Christ [be] in you, the body [is] dead because of sin; but the Spirit [is] life because of righteousness.* First, we see the Spirit of God taking up residence in the believer. This same Spirit seems to be the "Spirit of Christ." Moreover, 1 John 4:12 makes a clearer statement that "...God lives in us [believer]." To substantiate that the three in one also resides in the believer, Paul writes, *That Christ may dwell in your hearts by faith*, (Ephesians 3:17). Each born again person has the members of the Trinity residing in him. The fleshly body is considered a house or tabernacle of God, *What? know ye not that your body is the temple of the Holy Ghost [which is] in you, which ye have of God, and ye are not your own?* (1 Corinthians 6: 19)

The soul is in need of six additional spiritual elements as the flesh in order to function to its fullest potential.

We would see Jesus for Water

Like the body the soul needs to be refreshed. We read from the Gospel of John where Jesus discusses the matter of water with a young lady that came to draw from Jacob's Well: *But whosoever drink[s] of the water that I shall give him shall never thirst; but the water that I shall give him shall be in him a well of water springing up into everlasting life,* (John 4:14).

Since Jesus is living in the believer, the spiritual refreshing water is always present. The believer would be more positive, more apt to act out by faith if this one truth was taught more often. Many Christians see Christ as a savior outside and separate from the flesh. The topic of the indwelling Savior is revealed in Scripture as a mystery; although, it is one of the most reassuring doctrines revealed any believer can grasp. The union between the Spirit of God and the believer is totally voluntary for both parties concerned. Jesus said: *Behold, I stand at the door, and knock: if any men hear my voice, and open the door, I will come in to him, and will sup with him, and he with me* (Revelation 3:20). The repentant believer yields to the "knock" to accept Christ into his heart; accordingly, as promised, the Savior enters the body and soul of the believer: *But as many as received him, to them gave he power to become the sons of God, [even] to them that believe on his name* (John 1:12). Paul tells the Corinthians that this union would have remained a mystery if the Spirit had not instructed him to record this one doctrine.

Oliver B. Green stated, in part, in his *Commentary on the Gospel of John*: "The salvation which comes by grace through faith refreshes the believer as the flowing waters of a river refreshes a meadow through which it flows," (vol. I, 1976, p.214). Dr. Green is implying that there will always be a well within the believer where he can find refreshment when life becomes too dry, the world becomes too hot, or when the devil becomes too intense in his attacks. Since it is referred to as "living water," it resembles a bubbling fountain.

A person often needs a cool glass of water to drink after working in the hot sun. Subsequently, a person will feel refreshed and strengthened enough to continue his labor after drinking the water. Knowing the need of man, God supplied water from a rock in the Sinai Desert, (Exodus 17: 6; 1 Corinthians 10:4). Likewise, God knows our need for water in the Age of Grace.

PART TWO: SATISFYING MAN'S NATURAL AND SPIRITUAL NEEDS FOR HIS SOUL

Water serves the same two-fold purpose (refreshing and cleansing) for the soul as it does the body: *That he might sanctify and cleanse it with the washing of water by the word*, (Ephesians 5:26). The Greek word for water used in this verse presents the idea to cleanse. By reading the scripture a person can clean his thought-life before an evil presence can germinate it into sin: *Draw nigh to God, and he will draw nigh to you. Cleanse [your] hands, [ye] sinners; and purify [your] hearts* (James 4:8).

There are additional references that speak on the same subject. The word of God is seen as the river of water where the believer will be planted near by (Psalm 1:3). Jesus can be the still waters of Psalms 23; thus, the believer can find peace even when the enemy is close by. We would see Jesus for air and for water.

We would see Jesus for Food

And Jesus said unto them, I am the bread of life: he that cometh to me shall never hunger; and he that believeth on me shall never thirst, (John 6:35). Jesus was telling the Jewish community that He could provide everlasting life through faith in Him as Jehovah provided life for the forty years their fathers wondered in the desert. Besides, God provides the grain to be made into bread (*artos*) that promotes life for the flesh (Genesis 1:29). There were a number of Jewish Feasts that included bread. Before there was Showbread in the Holy Place, God gave the Hebrews manna from heaven to sustain them during their 40-year trek through the Sinai Desert. Both the Showbread in the Temple and manna in the wilderness are a type of Christ. The bread was unleavened which does not spoil, where as, yeast or bread with leaven can become spoiled with mold. Unleavened bread is used today in the more conservative Bible churches for the observance of the Lord's Supper. Since leaven or yeast represents sin throughout scripture, the symbols must coincide with God's character. This is the reason the wine used in the Lord's Supper is "new wine," or fresh juice from the grape before any fermentation developed.

Jesus states (John 6:51) that He was the "living bread that came down from heaven." Therefore, He was different from the manna from heaven since the Hebrew people, after eating manna, still died during their wanderings in the desert. Jesus promised everlasting life (John 6), if a person ate (accepted Him) as the new bread. Accepting the gift of forgiveness typifies eating Him, (taking Him spiritually into one's being) and in so doing, like the fountain of water, Jesus promised the believer he would no longer hunger or thrust. This meant Jesus would always sustain the believer. Elijah promised the widow that the flour used to make biscuits for him, her and her son would not be depleted as long as the Spirit of God remained on/in the home. Unlike the going and coming of the Holy Spirit in the Old Testament, once the Godhead takes up a spiritual residence in the believer's body, the New Covenant promises that God would never leave or forsake the believer.

When Jesus is allowed to live within, He brings salvation or life to the soul, which is sustaining life or eternal life. The reader has learned that Jesus is the Word of God, (John 1:1, 14). In the preceding paragraphs, the word is pictured as water of refreshment and cleansing. Presently, the word of God is pictured as food. This same food can be seen as milk for the newly converted: *As newborn babes, desire the sincere milk of the word, that ye may grow thereby:* (1 Peter 2:2). As one matures spiritually, drinking milk is replaced with eating bread, and then meat. To be sure, the soul of man will be satisfied with the nourishment Jesus promised to provide. We would see Jesus for air, water, and food for the soul.

We Would Also See Jesus for Rest/Sleep

I will both lay me down in peace, and sleep: for thou, LORD, only make[s] me dwell in safety (Psalm 4:8). David also speaks of rest, *He make[s] me to lie down in green pastures: he lead[s] me beside the still waters.* (Psalm 23:2) The Hebrew word used for peace is *shalom*. As the body needs to lay down to rest, the soul needs to experience a like period of peace – free from the pressures and cares of life. The believer needs to remember that wherever the body goes and whatever the body experiences, the soul/spirit experiences the same. The soul is linked to the mind, which includes an additional element within known as emotion. Thus, God knows the soul needs rest as much as the flesh. Jesus speaks of this rest, or peace, (*raynay*) found in John 14:27. He follows up this truth with: *These things I have spoken unto you, that in me ye might have peace* (16:33).

Jesus was trying to prepare the Apostles for troublesome times that were sure to come. Parents try to warn their children of possible dangers in order to save them undue suffering. Sometimes the children learn from their parents, but more often learning only comes through experience. When pain does come, parents stand close by to help their offspring endure the suffering. Likewise, Jesus is standing by the believer to give comfort. Comfort comes in the form of a good night's sleep or when inner peace settles upon the believer supernaturally.

The peace can come when we call upon Jesus to apply His peace (*eiphvu*), "We would see Jesus for Peace." If there is any single need in today's society it is peace to the soul. It will bring healing to the mind and body as well. Peace can prevent suicide and can bring tranquility to church congregations during trying times. One needs to see Jesus for air, water, food, and rest. The soul further needs a spiritual friend, spiritual ambition, and a spiritual love that is only understood in this metaphysical realm. We need to see Jesus for air, water, food, and rest.

We Would See Jesus for Friendship

Man was not meant to live a segregated life. God did not intend for the believer to cut himself off from society and live as a hermit. In fact, we can find Jesus walking among a portion of society that could be labeled "undesirable." Matthew stated that the Messiah was a friend of publicans and sinners, (Matthew 11:9). This is not to say that the off-scouring population adopted him as one of their own, but rather Jesus went out of His way to be their friend. Solomon wrote in order for a person to have friends that person must first show himself friendly, (Proverbs 18:2). This does not mean that Jesus took part in sin; He merely treated people with respect. He met them on their level in order to show a better way. He did not force Himself on them. He gave people a free will to make their own choice to accept His message of grace and forgiveness or to reject it. (The Pharisees criticized Jesus for being open to the common man, and they criticized John Baptist for living a separated life.)

The way Jesus approached the woman at the well shows His friendliness at work. He not only won the woman to Himself, His friendliness, in the beginning, was responsible for winning the town. Jesus was willing to converse with individuals in a non-judgmental way. By following this procedure, Matthew and Zaccheus were converted. Each man was shown his failure, his need to repent, and that his only hope was Jesus and none other. Once this was done, Jesus gladly accepted these persons once they desired change in their lives.

It must be pointed out that Jesus' critics said that He was a friend of publicans and sinners. By Christ's actions one can conclude a friendly approach was incorporated to win them. Because He had already chosen them as friends, He could finish His work by surrendering His life for them: *Greater love hath no man than this, that a man lay down his life for his friends. Ye are my friends,* (John 15:13-14). Please notice once more, who did the choosing. The sinner does not find God; on the contrary, God finds the sinner. In fact, man did not know he needed to be found, saved or redeemed until he learned of his lost condition.

The believer needs a person he or she can call a friend for several reasons. First, the believer retains his sin nature, and in so doing, will commit sin in the flesh. Therefore, the Christian needs someone to talk too and someone to pray for him. A friend should be an example the individual can look up to and trust. Second, the believer needs a spiritual friend because it is forbidden to make friends of the world to the extent in being identified with the unsaved person. Since the world had a curse placed on it from the time of the Garden of Eden, the world has become an enemy of God. Third, the believer needs a friend because Satan, even though he may appear to walk in the light, in reality, he walks in the shadows seeking someone to destroy, (1 Peter 5:8). Fourth, the believer needs a friend that sticks closer than a brother. A fellow Christian, sadly, could at any time turn their back upon the wayward – especially in times of trouble. This is due to the weakness of the flesh. A person, who turns his back on a brother or sister in need is not walking in the Spirit. The Apostles fled at the arrest of Jesus, and Peter denied the Savior three times when questioned. Mark left Paul early in the first missionary journey, and many other of Paul's companions scattered. The Apostle writes in 2 Timothy 4:10, that even Demas deserted him. The two promises that kept Paul on course were: *[Let your] conversation [be] without covetousness; [and be] content with such things as ye have: for he hath said, I will never leave thee, nor forsake thee.* And, *There hath no temptation taken you but such as is common to man: but God [is] faithful, who will not suffer you to be tempted above that ye are able; but will with the temptation also make a way to escape, that ye may be able to bear [it]* (1 Corinthians 10:13). The measure of a true friend is his willingness to stand by a person when that person is wrong. This is when an individual needs a friend – Jesus is that kind friend.

We need to see Jesus for air, water, food, rest, and friendship.

We Would See Jesus for Ambition

A synonym for ambition is motivation. Ambition is

seen many times as the fire or energy one has to get things done or the ability to accomplish a goal. Ambition is dependant on one's motivation, which is seen as the fuel used to produce the energy to work toward obtaining the desired goal.

Someone informed Zig Ziglar that he could not motivate anyone to do anything. The person was implying that Mr. Ziglar was merely creating the right climate and environment for the said person to be self motivated, (*Solving The Mystery of Motivation*, Carbonell, 1993). Hence, true motivation must come from within a person.

The Science of Human Behavior focuses on the part of the soul better known as the emotions. The Science of Psychology, in contrast, deals with abnormal behavior. The Science of Motivation, falling under the study of human behavior, considers the reasons a person feels and responds the way he does. Large corporations spend millions of dollars annually on books, seminars, and retreats for the purpose of increasing the company's revenue by increasing the worker's motivation to succeed in the stated business. People, who desire to advance in a company for economic purposes or for those who just wish to feel better about themselves, read books and listen to motivational tapes. The fastest growing trend today among counselors is for them to become a "life coach." A life coach merely assists people in discovering what they would like to do in life and then encourages them to take the proper steps in meeting the predetermined goals. It seems to be like having one's own personal cheerleader to talk too. Since Christians are people, they too may need a cheering section. It could be like the old fashion amen corner in the church; the more Amens the pastor hears, the harder he preaches.

Paul said, *Brethren, I count not myself to have apprehended: but [this] one thing [I do], forgetting those things which are behind, and reaching forth unto those things which are before, I press toward the mark for the prize of the high calling of God in Christ Jesus,* (Philippians 3:13-14). Even though Paul knew he had not reached the "mountain top" of success, he knew that he was heading in the right direction. He also saw an open-ended possibility: *"I can do all things through Christ, who will strengtheneth me,"* (Philippians 4:13). In verse nineteen, he relied upon Jesus for any success, and promised the church: *my God shall supply all* [our] *needs according to his riches in glory by Christ Jesus.*

PART TWO: SATISFYING MAN'S NATURAL AND SPIRITUAL NEEDS FOR HIS SOUL

As Jesus brings salvation to the soul, He implants an ambition to accomplish His purpose for the Kingdom of God. Jesus promised the believer, under His direction, would do greater works and produce abundant fruit. This becomes possible if the believer would only rely upon the Holy Spirit to direct his path.

What goals do you have in you life, for your family, for your church? Do you have a vision to see an x-amount of souls saved and baptized? Do you have a goal to read the Bible through this year, or to memorize several favorite chapters? Do you see yourself taking a college course just for self-fulfillment? Have you thought about writing a book or teaching a Sunday school class? All or any of these desires and more are possible when you see Jesus as a source of your strength. He never calls that He does not first give the ability to accomplish the task. We need to see Jesus for air, water, food, rest, friendship, and motivation.

We Would See Jesus for Love.

Regardless of the secular misunderstanding of the subject, there is one source that speaks at length on the topic of love. Three short texts that quickly come to mind are: (a) "For God so loved the world...(John 3:16); (b) "But God commended his love toward [the believer]...(Rom. 5:8); (c) "...God is love... (I John 4:8). The Bible is the source. There are almost 600 references for the word "love" and its variances listed in *Strong's Concordance*.

Stephen G. Post, professor of biomedical ethics and family medicine at Case Western Reserve University (Science & Theology News, Feb. 2004) notes that more than 100,000 scientific studies have been published on depression and schizophrenia, but no more than a dozen good studies have been published on unselfish love. Two million dollars in grants have been given to scholars recently to study the subject of love.

Bookstores are filled with romance novels. The major subject of women's magazines today is how to find and keep love/sex alive in one's life, not that sex and love are synonymous. Soap operas were developed to show the illicit pursuit of love even though a large percentage of the nation considers such affairs taboo or prohibited by most standards.

Ten's of thousands of sermons and lectures have been given on the subject of love. Dr. Wendell D. Mullen, former pastor of the First Baptist Church in Groton, Massachusetts, wrote a brief (unpublished) Bible study entitled, *Love Is A Bible Doctrine*. The fourteen chapters took a single aspect of love from God's prospective and related it to how the believer should develop the correct attitude of love for a fuller and richer relationship inside the church and for society.

When Jesus came to reside in the "Holy Place" of the soul of the believer, He brought the highest form of love (*agape*) with Him. This is the love that Christ asked Peter for, "Do you *agape* me Peter?" The Apostle in turn kept referring to the *phileo* type of love, (John 21:15), which is merely a fondness for another. However, when Jesus, in the person of the Spirit entered the believer, He brought all the love of God that was possible to bring. As a parent loves a child, God loves us and this love goes beyond mere finite understanding, *And to know the love of Christ, which passeth knowledge, that ye might be filled with* **all** [my emphasis] *the fullness of God*, (Ephesians 3:19). (The latter part of the verse speaks of being filled with **all** of God.) The fullness of God or the fullness of the Holy Spirit is completely there. It is not how much of God one receives; it is how much of the person God receives. Working in and under that filling is dependent upon man to first empty his soul of self; thus, allowing the presence of God to take control. The sooner the believer understands that God comes with love and will not allow evil or harmful hurt to come upon His child, the sooner the person will begin to exhibit heaven's unique power.

The love that is revealed is a sacrificial love, which is shown when Jesus took the place of the sinner on the cross, (Galatians 2:20; Ephesians 5:2). Because of this indwelling love the believer receives, he in turn, should walk in love. The world should witness this love the believer has for others: *There is no fear in love; but perfect love casteth out fear: because fear hath torment. He that feareth is not made perfect in love. We love him, because he first loved us. If a man say, I love God, and hateth his brother, he is a liar: for he that loveth not his brother whom he hath seen, how can he love God whom he hath not seen? And this commandment have we from him, That he who loveth God love his brother also.* (1 John 4:18-21). These four verses carry enough meat for a month of sermons.

Dr. Bill Pennell, formerly of Atlanta, Georgia, presented the following illustration on love in a morning message: *Anna*

Booth, the widow of William Booth who founded the Salvation Army, was returning home as the fog began to dim her path along the narrow street. Anna had just finished one of her neighborhood Bible studies. The elder saint saw a figure of a woman sitting on the sidewalk leaning against the pole of a street light. As Anna approached she concluded the woman's profession was of the immoral type due to the clothes she was wearing. As Mrs. Booth peered into the face of the frail-shivering figure sitting on the curb, she saw loneliness, sadness, and desperation. The girl let her head fall into her own hands that were resting on her knees. From the occasionally whimpers Anna heard, she knew there was distress lying heavily upon the young girl. Her clothes had been torn; bruises were evident on her bare shoulders and arms. From what part Anna could see of her face revealed scars common to a disease of her profession.

Mrs. Booth, tired from a day of witnessing and Bible studies, wished to continue home where a hot cup of tea and warm fire waited her arrival. Before moving down the street, she spoke to the young lady, "Jesus loves you," she said. But there was no response. Anna used a stronger voice and repeated the same claim. Silence filled the damp air. She added, "No matter what the problem, Jesus loves you more than you hate yourself." With this said, Anna began to resume her walk toward home. A muffled voice was heard say, "He is so far away," as the elder lady move

CHAPTER FIVE: SATISFYING MAN'S NATURAL AND SPIRITUAL NEEDS FOR HIS BODY AND SOUL

down the street with a tap of her cane.

Anna paused and asked the woman to repeat what she had said. Without looking up, the young lady repeated, "But Jesus is so far away." The old saint returned to take her original position next to the street light.

As she knelt down on the sidewalk next to the young lady, she said, "Jesus is closer than you think." Lifting the girl's face from her hands, Anna cradled her head in her own hands saying, "Jesus does love you and because He loves you and me, I love you with His love that is in my heart." She kissed her on the forehead and drew her to her bosom. Both ladies wept for some time before Anna offered hot tea and a warm fire and a clean bed to her newfound friend. "Besides," Anna whispered, "I can tell you more about the love of God." The finial scene was Anna and the young girl – walking arm in arm as they disappeared into the foggy night.

Have you experienced that love? Have you received the air that brings life? Have you drunk from the well that yields refreshing water for the soul? Have you feasted on the bread of life, and have you found rest in these troublesome times? Do you have a friend that will stand closer than a brother, even when you are wrong? Do you want ambition enough to see victories in your life? Do you

PART TWO: SATISFYING MAN'S NATURAL AND SPIRITUAL NEEDS FOR HIS SOUL

want to walk in love that will light the darkest of days? Come; let me introduce you to Jesus. It is He that you, and yes, all of society needs most.

As He has supplied the earth all the needs for the flesh, he will equally supply the same needs for the soul through Himself. Trust Him today and He will begin supplying the air, water, food and rest, as well as any ambition you may be lacking. He will be a true friend and love you with the purest love that heaven has to offer. It is all up to you! Say yes to Jesus. Ask Him to come into your heart/soul at this moment and all will be yours.

Let us pray: *Lord Jesus, I admit I am a sinner. There is a longing emptiness in my life that needs to be filled. I believe that Jesus came to earth to redeem mankind; I believe Jesus died on the cross of Calvary for my sin; I further believe that Jesus was buried and arose from the grave to proclaim everlasting life to whosoever will. The best I know how I am asking Christ Jesus to forgive me of my sin, and come into my heart with His loving salvation. Thank you, Lord, for saving my soul. Amen!*

CHAPTER FIVE: SATISFYING MAN'S NATURAL AND SPIRITUAL NEEDS FOR HIS BODY AND SOUL

Notes:

Benner, David, G., *Healing Emotional Wounds*. Michigan: Baker Book House, 1990.

Carbonell, Mells (Ph.D.), *Solving the Mystery of Motivation*. Fayetteville, Georgia: Institute of Leadership Technology. 1993.

Carrington, W.L. (M.D.), *Psychology, Religion, and Human Need*. New York: Channel Press, 1957.

Collins, John, *Christian Counseling*. Dallas: Word Publishing, 1988.

Dryer, Wyne, *The Sky's the Limit*. New York: Simon and Schuster, 1980.

Green, Oliver, B., *Commentary on the Gospel of John vol. I*. Greenville, South Carolina: The Gospel Hour, Inc., 1966.

Harris, William H., and Levey, Judith, S., (Eds.) The New *Columbia Encyclopedia*. New York: Columbia University Press, 1995.

Thiessen, Henry, C., *Introductory Lectures in Systematic Theology*. Michigan: Wm. B. Eerdmans Publishing Company, 1975.

Vine, W.W. (M.A.) *An Expository Dictionary of New Testament Words*. Nashville: Thomas Nelson, Publishers.

— CHAPTER SIX —

AN ANALOGY OF SPIRITUAL ANEMIA

What is anemia? Anemia is a medical condition in humans defined as a deficiency in one or more elements of the blood. It is a condition in which the blood is in such poor quality that it does not carry enough nutrients to keep the body in good repair. The result is that the sufferer becomes thin, pale, lifeless, and lacks strength and energy. Because of a poor appetite, which often accompanies anemia, the physical defenses are broken enough that the individual is prone to catch an array of diseases to which the person is exposed.

I will ascribe the physical anemia that occurs in the body to the lack of spiritual energy that should fill the soul and vice versa. The reader has learned from the essay above that God has supplied all the needed ingredients for both

CHAPTER SIX: AN ANALOGY OF SPIRITUAL ANEMIA

body and soul. (See *Satisfying Man's Natural and Spiritual Needs for His Body and Soul*) When a Christian taps into the stated resources, he will be able to live an abundant life. The problem of spiritual anemia arises in areas of the spirit and the flesh when the believer fails to realize the availability of the needed nutrients that are found in Jesus Christ. I have always taught that Jesus, in His death on the cross, made a "spiritual transfusion" possible. Man's tainted blood was inherited from his ancestral father, Adam. Scripture tells us that we are unable to save ourselves, not to mention another soul, since we are just as polluted with sin as the person in question. The Bible further reveals that nothing can be substituted in place of the transfusion that Christ offers. Salvation with the forgiveness of sin only comes through Christ: *I am the way, the truth, and the life, no man [can come] unto the Father but by me* (John 14:6). We have life due to the blood (Genesis 9:4; Leviticus 17:14). Leviticus presents a vivid analogy of the cross: *[F]or the life of the flesh is in the blood: and I have given it to you upon the altar [cross] to make an atonement for your souls: for it is the blood that make[s] an atonement for the soul* (v.11). In conjunction, the author of Hebrews states in chapter nine that Jesus Christ became the atonement or the One who gave His blood in order that the human race might be spared the

CHAPTER SIX: AN ANALOGY OF SPIRITUAL ANEMIA

second death or the lake of fire. Since Jesus had pure blood, absent of Adam's sin, due to the virgin birth (Luke 1:34-38), He could freely offer you and me the needed transfusion.

The believer's strength comes from reading God's word, praying, and keeping himself unspotted from the world. Consequently, the Christian can become thin and impoverished with scarcely enough vitality to keep his or her soul empowered enough for the work God has called the believer to do. Because of this spiritual poverty, the church is becoming spiritually weaker as this dispensation slides further into the Laodicean era (Revelation 3:14-22). A growing number of Christian pastors believe that the church's evangelical work and influence is growing less affective as the days go by. Thus, the weakened soul lacks the resistance to turn from false teachers and doctrines of devils. The *social gospel* is becoming more socially accepted by appealing more to the flesh than the spirit. Spiritual members of the church believe they are witnessing at least one cause for this weakened condition. They see more seeds of the Eastern philosophy being accepted by the general population. Sadly, this philosophy is spilling over into the church at a greater rate than before. In addition, I have witnessed more apathy toward living a pure Christian life among the general membership than ever before; mainly, because Christians have been reconditioned to accept a weaker gospel. Paul warned Timothy (paraphrasing), The time would come when men would be lovers of themselves, covetous, proud, boasters, generally disobedient, unthankful, unholy, and down right blasphemous, etc., (2 Timothy 3:2-7).

Secondly, we are currently seeing a "falling away" from the things of God that is caused, in my opinion, by consistent demonic attacks that has diverted the Christian's attention from God to himself and the world. Because of the coldness toward God from the people of God, due to the spiritual backsliding, it is reasonable to expect the disease of spiritual anemia to be laced throughout the churches and communities of this nation.

Society, in contrast, has given itself over to becoming healthy in body. Every branch of the media are flooding the airways and printed pages with advertisements for pills, diets, organic foods, and exercise machines, all of which promise a healthier body. Every diet or workout is supposed to help increase the flow of blood through the body. The theory states that a splendid circulatory system is the body's best defense. This is true. When a full volume of well

Chapter Six: An Analogy of Spiritual Anemia

fortified blood journeys throughout the body as a free-flowing mountain stream, it not only gives more life to every organ, it also purifies the organs that are supposed to keep the person healthy. This is likewise true for the prosperity of the soul. Both physical and spiritual barriers can be set up against every foul invasion the devil or the world can throw in the believer's direction. This is the reason Christians must be alert to the devil's devices. The devil will wage an attach against the believer by inflicting numerous kinds of diseases that will attack both body and mind. He will use the enticements of the world to further misdirect the Christian's attention from the real cause for his weakness. He will attack his mind and emotions – anything to stop the believer from thinking about God and His work He wishes him to do, and/or his dependence on Him for his daily needs.

A number of my Christian friends and I have discussed many of the problems this country is currently facing. In fact, these same problems can been seen in countries around the world. For example, we have witnessed increased violence, senseless brutality, and mass slayings on a daily basis. Such harsh attacks are tearing at the heart strings of a number of communities. Moreover, there is a

CHAPTER SIX: AN ANALOGY OF SPIRITUAL ANEMIA

general unrest among other countries in that they seem to despise the overt philosophy of America. Our discussion seemed to always fall around to what is not being heard in today's average church that should strengthen the believer. We concluded there is a plague of spiritual anemia falling over the Christian population. The anemic condition could explain much of the weakness and many of the maladies Christian churches seemed to be experiencing. A few pastors are bewildered, but they seem clueless on how to correct the situation. I do not know what they learned from their homiletic class, but it seems that the new generation of pastors does not radiate the same fire and energy in the pulpit as their ancestors did a generation ago. In my opinion, I have heard only a few messages that would bring true conviction or repentance to any congregant. One seldom hears the word sin, devil, or hell ever mentioned in the pastor's *talk*. Pastors may have either been instructed in their homiletic class or informed by the deacons that such messages would drive people away. A sermon on hell and repentance was the topic the night I trusted Jesus Christ as my Lord and Savior. Revivals were common place in the mid-50s and before. The preacher of yesteryear did not *mix words* or tone down his messages. In other words, he preached what the Bible said and let the chips fall where

CHAPTER SIX: AN ANALOGY OF SPIRITUAL ANEMIA

they would. Consequently, it is not like that in quite a number of pulpits across this land today. I recently heard a pastor literally apologize to his congregation before his sermon because he was going to use the word "hell" several times in the morning message.

A few years ago the Holy Spirit revealed to me that my messages were beginning to sound like what a neo-evangelical would present. I was not preaching error, but the sermons were not anointed with fire/power as the earlier ones were. As I look back over the sermons, I found myself targeting the intellectual rather than the lost or the troubled. The devil is very crafty in the way he will influence a pastor to change his message as not to offend anyone. Yesterday's sermons will turn into messages; messages then will evolve into mere lectures tomorrow. At this level of decent, there will be little resistance for a lecture to shift into merely a Sunday talk. These talks may not even refer to God or His promises. Scripture from the Bible may not even be referenced. (Thank God the Holy Spirit revealed my trend of descent in time for me to make the proper correction.) The longer one remains on the declining path leading away from God, the more pronounced it will become. Before the pastor realizes his position or attitude, his ministry would have fallen deeper into liberalism. Once there, the minister will find it less likely or almost impossible to return to a more conservative footing. In fact, there is overwhelming evidence that comes from the study of apologetics that says, "Once a person leaves one camp, such as neo-evangelicalism and moves left into neo-orthodoxy, that person seldom, if ever, returns to the former camp of belief and practice."

There are seven stages of theological thought: fundamentalism and neo-fundamentalism; evangelicalism and neo-evangelicalism; orthodoxy and neo-orthodoxy; liberalism and neo-liberalism; socialism, Communism, and chaos. Each stage moves further left in philosophical thought until there is nothing left for the lost society to hear. This is possible the era when the "survival of the fittest" becomes a reality.

This brings me to my second opinion for the reason there is a spiritual anemic virus working its way through the Christian landscape. The average pastor is afraid he will be accused of not being friendly if he names sin as the Bible does. A number of pastors fear the governing board of the church, which has the power to fire for one reason or for none. Judging sermons, in most cases, is very

CHAPTER SIX: AN ANALOGY OF SPIRITUAL ANEMIA

subjective. It comes down on how much power the deacons or church board retains. Preaching like the founding ministers during the early years of the nation may be considered too scary for women and children today.

Paul told the Corinthian Church that he did not want his preaching to be described as wind chimes (1 Corinthians 13:1). He also forewarned Timothy that the day would come when congregations would ask the pastors to tone down their messages. *For the time will come when they [church] will not endure sound doctrine...having itching ears...they shall turn away their ears from the truth and shall be turned unto fables,* (2 Timothy 4:3-4). It would be like a doctor deluding a person's medication of its potency because it either had a bad taste or because it would bring on a stinging sensation.

I had the same fears or concerns that strong preaching would hinder people from staying in the church until a dear old saint shared a truth she had learned from experience, "There may have to be a blessed subtraction (people exiting the church) she called "dead wood" before God can bring a biblical addition to the work of God." The saint's view on how God had worked in her generation reminded me of how

CHAPTER SIX: AN ANALOGY OF SPIRITUAL ANEMIA

God worked in Bible times. Gideon's army was cut from 32,000 men to 300 men. Moreover, Jesus called many but only a few decided to follow. We have to remember that the battle is not ours, but the Lord's. You, I, and the Lord make up the majority.

Thank God older Christians have remained faithful to their churches. These faithful few are the first to admit the sermons seemed to have turned into positive psychological messages that contain a mere touch of scripture. The pastors' energy seemed to have waned; they have failed to challenge the church to contend for the faith as Jude encouraged the next generations to do. There is little vision, venture, vim or verger left in the present generation to lead the church into the 21st Century. All ministries do not fall under this category. There are some works that are doing a superb job; yet, scores of other churches appear in need of a transfusion. (The reader can "**Google**" or search **Barna.com** for current trends in modern Christianity. Do not be surprised what you will find.) For example:

> According to "Biblical Illiteracy Spreading Among Christians," (http://news.CrossWalk.com) the Program for International Student Assessment, a

CHAPTER SIX: AN ANALOGY OF SPIRITUAL ANEMIA

group who does surveys in several different areas and subjects, found that thirty-two industrialized countries, including America, showed a below average knowledge of biblical facts. Church leaders are using the phrase "dangerously low" instead of "totally illiterate" when biblical knowledge is concern to lessen the severity of the problem. Could the reason be due to the church leader's own anemic condition? The lack of biblical knowledge in the present generation means that the majority of congregations lacked text comprehension. When a large number of a congregation fails to understand the basic meaning of major Bible verses, the church becomes vulnerable to a number of spiritual attacks and shams of the world. [The lack of knowledge can vary from church to church.]

George Barna (Barna Research Online: "Religious Beliefs Vary Widely by Denomination") found that mainline Protestant denominations are fading in basic biblical doctrine that deals with the deity of Jesus Christ and the morality of its members; the reliability of the Bible; and how to get to

Chapter Six: An Analogy of Spiritual Anemia

heaven (works – vs – grace). The question that rated the lowest response revealed that the average church member did not believe in the reality of Satan. Among Baptist, statistics showed that only 34% actually believed in the reality of Satan but 66% believed in the accuracy of the Bible, but half of those questioned could not understand the reason Jesus must be without sin. This is truly alarming! What happen to people's belief? How could a nation, founded on Christian principles just over 200 years ago, fall to such a low standard of belief? America is standing on the brink of a total social and religious collapse if the statistics are not soon turned around. (June 25, 2001).

A number of resources detail some of the reasons Christianity's image is slipping among America's younger population. A recent survey among 16 to 29 year olds revealed that the younger generation is more skeptical and resistant to Christianity than were people the same age a mere decade ago. Those surveyed, religious and nonreligious, seemed to be highly critical of major religions. The hardest hit by their mistrustfulness were the evangelicals.

CHAPTER SIX: AN ANALOGY OF SPIRITUAL ANEMIA

Evangelicals are Christians who openly witness to the lost world with the hope to turn some to salvation. There is a sense among evangelical Christians that the world population is becoming more hostile and negative toward Christianity. Christian pastors tend to agree that building a church through evangelism has become more difficult today than a decade ago. And growing number of the population in a given community do not want a church to be built in their neighborhood.

What seems to be the problem? Could it be that God is fading in the average Christian's life to the point, he or she has lost the power to overcome spiritual resistance in accepting the Christian faith? (Accepting Christ as Savior by faith is only the beginning of the believer's walk. The believer needs daily faith in order to continue his journey. Spiritual anemia develops when faith begins to slip.) Has Christian America failed in its ideals to maintain an influence over the government, the educational system, and the church to keep a strong enough moral attitude in place in order to prevent hardening of the hearts of men and women against moral wrong? Has the American secular sector educated its citizens from believing in a living God?

CHAPTER SIX: AN ANALOGY OF SPIRITUAL ANEMIA

I believe so! God is, indeed, fading from the lives of Christian citizens in general to the point that two out of three adults or 66% contend that religion is losing its influence in American's society, (Barna, 2003). Currently, a high percentage of Christians believe that all forms of immorality, adultery, homosexuality, pornography, gambling and other carnal activity are morally acceptable behavior today than in the last 500 years.

One may argue from the point that scores of churches are growing, but this growth is not a reliable sign of spirituality. There are more mega churches than ever before. A mega church means having 2,000 or more attendees in a single service. Those who sense a growing spiritual emptiness in the general church member have developed their own statistics. For example, over half of the faithful view the church loosing its influence in the local community. Church members themselves have stated that they do not see any problem with America's churches. The majority of church goers believe they were growing deeper in the Lord, but these same people testified that they were not only reading the Bible less and praying less, they were less involved in church activities. Moreover, there has been less of an impact among the community because of fading Christians even

CHAPTER SIX: AN ANALOGY OF SPIRITUAL ANEMIA

though they continue to sit in the pew each week. Most of the faithful believe that if the churches were doing their job, pure reason would conclude that moral sin would not be on the rise like it is. According to the FBI reports murders jumped 4.8 percent in the year 2000; robberies increased 4.5 percent, and jail populations are bulging with an annual additional of 34,000 inmates, on average.

The church is too often characterized by the unfailing symptom of anemia. Some believe the failure to adjust oneself to the new and unfamiliar could be the cause. The body of the church as well as many pastors and staff has been slow in seeing opportunity or even the weakened condition of the present day believer. I call this condition, an "ostrich syndrome;" if one doesn't see a problem, there must be no problem to correct. Therefore, scores of people will continue to hide their head in the preverbal sand while the devil deludes yet another community of believers. Overcoming denial is often the first step leading to correcting any problem – drug addition, alcoholism, pornography, etc.

The question must be restated: What brought about the anemic condition in the Christian church? To answer this important question with the aspect of correcting the

CHAPTER SIX: AN ANALOGY OF SPIRITUAL ANEMIA

illness, one should contrast the physical anemia with the spiritual anemia. For example (not in chronological order of importance), the spiritual anemic person is "run down." Society has developed a busy run-run lifestyle for its citizens. The spiritual individual, like the secular person, has become too busy with living. The average Christian has too much on his plate to spend time with God. The secular American citizen does not make time to spend quality time with his or her family. Hundreds, if not thousands of people, fail to make enough time for a physical exam until ill health puts them in an emergency room at the hospital. On the flip side scores of people are busy becoming healthy physically while they become spiritually weaker on a daily basis.

The devil has not actually changed his objective which is the total destruction of mankind, who is representative of God's image. Instead of an overt and/or frontal attack, the devil is adding distraction to his slate of curricula. He has not given up his sly tactic of postponing salvation until a later date; he has merely added a new weapon to wage against the average Christian home and church. God's invitations seemingly have gone unnoticed today because we are too busy or distracted to hear His *still small voice*. Society and the church are not quiet/still enough

Chapter Six: An Analogy of Spiritual Anemia

to hear heaven's plea. Being overly busy in church work is not necessarily a show of godliness or spirituality.

Teachers who work with students that have attention deficient disordered (ADD) are always repeating their instructions because such over active brains are never quiet long enough to hear the lesson plan the first-time around. I am sure the reader can easily recall a number of persons that could fit under the heading of ADD. In addition, hundreds of pastors fail to take breaks from the ministry to remain fresh. If a pastor does not take time off, he cannot be a proper example to his congregation. My professors kept warning us preacher boys that we had better schedule time to come apart from the ministry or we would literally come apart. In the language modern society can understand, pastors need to press the pause button ever so often. In addition, the question must be asked, "How many pastors have told their congregations that God gave him this morning's message this past week?" Or, does the pastor use an annual registry of sermon outlines, written by who knows who and how many years ago, to set the spiritual aptitude of *his congregation*? Or was it used to free him for his monthly game of golf?

CHAPTER SIX: AN ANALOGY OF SPIRITUAL ANEMIA

All Christians need to keep an on-going close relationship with God. To do this, the believer needs to find a quite time to read the Bible and to pray. For reference one should study the Gospels to find the times Jesus withdrew Himself to a quite place (Luke 5:16). God will not compete with the noise of the world nor will He try to speak when man is speaking. John Baptist literally separated himself from the rustle and bustle of society. Moses spent 40 days upon Mount Sinai receiving the Ten Commandments and another 40 days gaining instruction on how to construct the Tabernacle. Paul, already a religious leader, took three years in the back side of the desert to restudy the Old Testament Scriptures that spoke of Jesus Christ as the Messiah. Likewise, John, the beloved, sat in silence on the Isle of Patmos where he received the greatest end-time prophecy ever presented.

The third reason churches could be filled with anemic Christians is that modern believers desire an instant God where their worship time resembles a drive-through eatery. The spiritual anemic person has no problem driving across the state for a rock concert; and he will feel cheated if the concert does not last at least three or four hours. The same person will complain if he has to drive across town to attend church. He further becomes quite annoyed if the

Chapter Six: An Analogy of Spiritual Anemia

sermon goes five minutes over time. The spiritual anemic often attends a church where more emphasis is placed on the music program than the message of God. (There should be a balance between music and message. The type of music falls under another category). It appears that the Sabbath has been changed to mean a time for recreation instead of a time of rest and meditation.

Modern appliances were developed to save us time and energy for more meaningful things in life, such as, reading a book or enjoying a meal with the entire family with no television or radio playing in the background. Such family relationships are dissolving because the devil and his hoard are distracting man from worshiping God properly. How did we communicate with our friends and family before cell phones and text messages? Do we need to talk as much as we do? Church congregations have to be reminded, over and over again, to turn their cell phones off before the service. And only God knows how many silent texts are being sent during the service.

When God begins to fade from a person's life, the evaporation in most cases becomes a hurried downhill process and will affect on going generations if the loss is not stopped. It can happen in a short period of time. Abraham was called by God to father a new nation that would carry the message of salvation to the world. God was **God** to Abraham; and we learned from scripture that Abraham became God's Friend. The next generation continued in Isaac, but God only became "an Awe for Isaac," not a close friend. Jacob, the third generation that worshiped Jehovah as God, did not retain Isaac's *Awe* of God, nor was he a personal friend of God even though Jacob was responsible for bringing the Twelve Tribes of Israel into being. We remember him because he stole his brother's birthright, and he had to work extra years in order to marry the woman he loved. Jacob had to have a makeover due to his fading relationship with God. Once the makeover was underway, beginning at *the ladder leading to heaven*, Jacob had to deal with his anemic backslidden condition following his second encounter by wrestling the Angle of God. He concluded a life change was needful. Once fellowship between him and Jehovah was renewed, God was able to change Jacob's name to Israel – the *supplanter* became the man that obtained power with God. Jehovah was then able to bless him many times over because he was once again a productive witness and a faithful follower. Consequently, God has been fading from the minds and hearts of my generation for a

CHAPTER SIX: AN ANALOGY OF SPIRITUAL ANEMIA

long while, but it appears the rate of retreat is slowing. A number of pastor's conferences are beginning to use the "R" word – *Revival*, the word that has not been used in its proper context for over 40 years. (Pastors need to relay the same concern for the need of revival to their churches.) Conservative believers are encouraged to learn that a few "seeker friendly" ministries are gradually changing back to a more conventional topical service. Regional surveys have found that seeker members lack basic biblical knowledge. The goal is now to gradually preach more theologically or more biblically rather than spiting out a psychological feel-good-about-yourself rhetoric.

I do not believe I will be taking scripture out of context with the following illustration. Please visualize Nebuchadnezzar's image from the Book of Daniel. I would like to compare spiritual fading by way of the metals that made up the statue. The statue was composed of four different metals that represented four individual nations or empires that would dominate world history: Babylon, Medes and Persians, Greece, and Rome. The head made of gold, the softest of the four metals, represented the great Babylonian empire. The next element was silver found in the two arms represented the Medes and the Persians. Silver

CHAPTER SIX: AN ANALOGY OF SPIRITUAL ANEMIA

is still quite valuable, but a degree harder than gold. The area around the waste of the image was made of a brass alloy. Like Jacob, brass was only third removed from the head of gold, but already there was an evident difference. Brass is a component of metals made from cooper and zinc. This means the third position was made of a mixture of other metals. A close fellowship can be equated with the head of gold. Fading in value to silver typifies the change seen in the second metal. The population that represents the brass section has become even more of a mixed alloy in their thinking; thus, a mixture that led to a harder substance but lass valued than the former two. The final metal found in the two legs and feet was iron. It is the sturdiest, but the iron is forth removed from gold. The people of Rome that represent the section of iron were war like and had no relationship with the Spirit of God. Their own strength replaced God's wooing Spirit. At this stage it seems impossible to be renewed as seen in the clay trying to mix or become part of the iron in the feet of the image. This typifies the last generation before God descends to judge humanity. As God fades from man's environment, he becomes less valued: from gold to iron. As time goes on, man will fill the void with mixed material as a substitute for God. The further mankind moves from the throne room (royal gold), he has to

CHAPTER SIX: AN ANALOGY OF SPIRITUAL ANEMIA

compensate his loss of radiance by adopting the world's alloy of intellectualism and secularism; thus, man increases his personal strength but looses the iridescence of a spiritual relationship. Spiritually, the believer has moved from the *Shekinah Glory* (the presence of God) found in the Holy of Holies to being entirely separated from God outside the camp.

Please allow me point out an aspect that may have been overlooked. God never moves; it is always man that moves away from God. James tells the believer to, *Draw nigh to God, and He will draw nigh to you*....(James 4:8). When the believer begins to wander away from God, he or she begins the process of having God fade from the Christian's life. It is like taking an ember from a fire. Heat immediately begins leaving the ember because the energy is not self-contained. If the ember is moved further way from the source of heat, it will loose its burning ability at a faster rate until at some point it will no longer retain any warmth whatsoever. Likewise, the anemic will become more harden as the days go by like the iron of the image. In addition, his spirit will become cooler toward the things of God the further he wonders from the source of power.

CHAPTER SIX: AN ANALOGY OF SPIRITUAL ANEMIA

Unfortunately, God has begun fading from our minds and hearts as illustrated above. Most scholars believe we are presently living in the end times (when Christendom/society turns to iron). *Wherefore the Lord said, Forasmuch as this people draw near me with their mouth, and with their lips do honor me, but have removed their heart far from me...*(Isaiah 29:13). The prophet is describing a people who worship God dishonestly. This will bring on the condition of anemia. If Christians fail to keep God centered in their lives, the Person of the Holy Spirit will be grieved, so much so, that His power will diminish at a faster rate than ever before. Man's spiritual fading will affect not only himself, but churches, communities and eventually the nation. The solution is to renew one's relationship with God. This is done by drawing close to God who promises that He will keep you company through life's ups and downs. When the believer grows cold toward God, the Holy Spirit will become grieved to the point no spiritual work will be possible. Jesus could not perform any great work in cities where unbelief reigned. Moreover, fading implies a process. Satan will not identify himself as Satan nor his angels as demons when they bring temptations to modern man. Satan did not approach Eve as a nasty fire breathing dragon in the Garden, but came as a gentle reasoning soft-spoken walking serpent.

CHAPTER SIX: AN ANALOGY OF SPIRITUAL ANEMIA

Neither will God turn His back on the first offence of His children. He is a loving God who wishes no one to perish. He remained approachable for 120 years while Noah constructed the Ark. The prophet Ezekiel pictures the Holy Spirit withdrawing from Jerusalem in steps. The Holy Spirit, in the first step, removed Himself from between the cherubims on the Mercy Seat and stood at the threshold of the House of God. The Spirit then moves from the doorway to the Mount of Olives; from there He ascended from the nation of Israel. Without the presence of the power of God, it allowed the judgment of God to fall (Ezekiel 10:1-22). The Lord warns the Church of Ephesus to repent or she will loose her candlestick, which means that the power and presence of God will be taken (Revelation 2:5). In other words, the church would not retain the presence and power of God.

The presence of God began to fade in the heart of David under several temptations of Satan. But David came to himself and repented of his past actions and grave sin. Because of David's renewed spirit and repentant heart, unlike King Saul, David is still known today as the *apple of God's eye*. Consequently, we see God fading in David's son, Solomon. He did not learn from his father's failures. History records that "King Solomon loved many strange women." God warned the entire nation of Israel about taking strange (unbelieving) women to marry. David had over 300 such wives, but Solomon had 700 foreign wives. The scriptures tell us: *that his wives turned away his heart after other gods: and his heart was not perfect with the Lord his God, as was the heart of David his father* (1 Kings 11:2). The text goes on to say that God had faded in the heart of Solomon to the point that the King who asked for and was granted great wisdom, constructed high places or worship areas in order for his wives to have a place to burn incenses and sacrifice unto false gods. (There is a similar action taking place in America, not between the President and foreign women, but between America's court system and the *strange* nation of Islam.)

America will find herself destine for judgment if the fading of the knowledge of God continues, (Romans 1:8). The Bible says, *Righteousness exalt[s] a nation but sin is a reproach to any people* (Proverbs 14:34). David wrote in Psalms 9:17: *...any nation will be turned into hell that forgets God.* (America is beginning to forfeit her testimony before God by taking "In God We Trust," from her money. Thankfully, only a few pieces have the phrase, "In God We Trust" miniaturized so no one will notice the fading of God

CHAPTER SIX: AN ANALOGY OF SPIRITUAL ANEMIA

when the testimony is no longer present.) In addition, the Supreme Court has reinterpreted the U.S. Constitution to place a chasm between the church and state. The Court has ruled that prayer cannot be voiced in many public places, and the Ten Commandments cannot be publicly displayed while at the same time they can be found on a number of state buildings. Contrary to fact, on the eastern pediment of the Supreme Court building, one can not but notice the central figure is the biblical Moses, the chief law giver of all time. Furthermore, the Ten Commandments are displayed on the wall inside the Supreme Courtroom to the right of the sitting magistrates.

The city of Washington D.C. is filled with religious or Bible references in plane view of the public. For example, one panel found in the Jefferson Memorial reads: "We hold there truths to be self-evident: that all men are created equal, that they are endowed by their Creator with certain inalienable rights." A second panel begins with the words, "Almighty God hath created the mind free..." and concludes with, "... the plan of the Holy Author of our religion...." Moreover, the Founding Fathers were men of faith. George Washington wrote, "Thou gavest Thy Son to die for me; and has given me the assurance of salvation, upon my repentance and sincerely endeavoring to conform my life to His holy precept and example." Washington further encouraged every officer under his command, "...to live and act as [it] becomes a Christian soldier defending the dearest rights and liberties of his country." James Madison, the fourth United States President, said that the members of the first U.S. Congress instituted a self-governing body by the people based on the Ten Commandments. Both John Adams and John Hancock agreed by applying their signature to the statement, "We recognize no sovereign but God, and no king but Jesus." Before July 4th, 1776, every session of the Congress began with a prayer and the practice of opening this governing body with prayer by a member of the clergy continues to this day.

The illustrations given above, when included in a sermon, are considered strong preaching by many today. A preacher who delivers such a "wake-up call" for the church must have true grit or conviction mixed with compassion. Modern pastors do not wish to preach such a negative message (so-called), nor does the average congregation wish to listen for fear they would fall under conviction and have to change their beliefs and lifestyle. Such individuals should ask themselves, if they want the medical doctor to tell them the truth or sugarcoat the enviable. The average church member

CHAPTER SIX: AN ANALOGY OF SPIRITUAL ANEMIA

is unable to concentrate or to comprehend a true relationship with God due to Him fading from the believer's life.

I believe the church has steadily moved "left" in the wake of the world. What was once considered sin is now merely a disorder or has been downgraded to an opinion to soften its hazardous poison? A drunkard has been renamed an alcoholic. Instead of showing the dangers of drinking, the community has been sold the idea of assigning designated drivers. Colorful billboards show the different brands of alcohol and the life of enjoyment drinking can bring, but fail to show broken families and dead bodies on the highway that alcohol has caused. Adultery has been relabeled an affair. The media is selling the idea that affairs are normal among humanity. This is after the liberals took the book of morality out of the classrooms, and in so doing, denied the existence of God. School curriculum no longer reinforces moral values. When an individual or nation forgets God, sin will be set aside as being antiquated; without sin there will not be any guilt; without guilt there will be no judgment; without judgment there will be no hell. But society and the high courts can not be able to erase the precepts of God, (Palms 119:89). The media and Hollywood may rename their programs "family television," but they continue to

CHAPTER SIX: AN ANALOGY OF SPIRITUAL ANEMIA

show adult content: *Sex In The City, Desperate Housewives, Girls Next Door, Bad Girls, Nip & Tuck,* and a number of "reality shows" to name a few.

We, who sense an anemic condition throughout the church and much of Christendom, must start overtly voicing concern. If spiritual anemia is allowed to continue, the church will soon be too weak to be effective enough to care for the ill and the dying in a cursed world. We need to remember that a sick person generally will not feel like eating; the spiritual vanquished will tend to reject any assistance. It is little use to treat anemia in a shallow way. The pick-me-up power drinks will only bring temporary relief of sluggishness to the body. Anemia will require more than a quick-fix. The *backslidden* person needs a longer lasting cure. A person may become excited enough to begin correcting his walk merely to run out of gas halfway to the goal. Churches need to organize a group of spiritual coaches to circumvent this very trend. Spiritual pep rallies with exciting, yet biblical speakers should be held often to keep the church encouraged and excited. Correcting spiritual anemia will require more than a "drive through" Sunday prayer or attending services two Sundays in a row. Spiritual anemia comes from a neglected and perverted relationship

Chapter Six: An Analogy of Spiritual Anemia

that has its roots tied to the flesh and the world. Such a relation must be corrected or severed before one's health can be restored. We tend to forget that the sought after relationship is between man and God, the Creator of the universe. The person must further take into consideration when his relationship with Jesus Christ needs to be refined. Some health problems will only require a few pills or a convicting sermon, while another person may require surgery, major dialysis, or a complete life change.

One problem seems to be that many Christians are like children – wanting to take the easiest way out. Those who wish to restore health and/or relationships will tend to take the road that has least resistance, mainly because the average anemic has quenched the power of the Holy Spirit so long that the road to recovery will be long and laborious. Visualize a husband offering only flowers to his wife following a major argument. On the other hand, the wife will try going down the same road of recovery/reconciliation by preparing her husband's favorite meal. Both of these acts are needful and appreciated, but neither party seems willing to sit down and discuss what caused the dispute in the first place. Therefore, the weak area in their marriage will remain fractured until the couple is willing to delete the old program

Chapter Six: An Analogy of Spiritual Anemia

and install an up-to-date marriage program that includes God.

There is always the possibility a number of anemic Christians will try to do the same type of reconciling tactics with God as did the wife and husband above. For example, the Christian who realizes there has been a break in relationship between him and God, for whatever reason (sin, denial, or neglect), will try to make amends or ease their conscious. They may try reading a whole chapter from the Bible, saying a generic prayer, or by attending church once or twice in a row. Others may try to appease God by putting a little extra in the offering plate. Such persons do not wish to surrender totally, admit the wrong, or truly repent by turning from and denying the sin and coldness of his or her heart. Most people fail to realize, if a main channel leading to and from the heart is blocked, it may require surgery, a life-change or a complete makeover. If proper corrections are not made, it will not only cause further ill health, a more weakened spirit; but, in many cases, it could lead to a premature death.

How can spiritual anemia be corrected? (This topic will be discussed further in detail later.) The partial secret, only because we fail to recognize the solution, is found in the spiritual text book: "He that drinks my blood hath life."

CHAPTER SIX: AN ANALOGY OF SPIRITUAL ANEMIA

(Christians do not drink literal blood. The text is speaking figuratively when one accepts the death of Christ on the cross.) This is the beginning cure for spiritual anemia. Our blood at present is weak. The old blood that is pumped out goes through the dialysis of Jesus Christ before it is replaced in the body. The new blood has all the nutrients needed to first repair damaged cells that caused the believer's impotence, and second, energize him or her enough to return to the community with good news.

David acknowledged the need to be re-energized (Psalm 85:6), "Will you not revive us again...?" (Amplified) The King of Israel made several positive statements in Psalm 23. Because of the love of God, David or any believer would not be in want; the believer will rest in green pastures beside peaceful waters; and he will be advised of the correct path to take – all because God restored his soul. In other words, faith in Jesus Christ will produce an abundant life. When the spiritual blood becomes tired, it will be replaced with good energy that will awaken sleeping faculties and arouse dormant abilities of expression that will lead to wondrous works and miraculous ministries. Because of God's accuracies in mercy and forgiveness, David was able to confess his greatest sin in Psalm 51.

CHAPTER SIX: AN ANALOGY OF SPIRITUAL ANEMIA

If each spiritual anemic person would adopt David's plan, the entire church would be able to change her weak, tired, and sluggish existence to one of rejuvenation. Change must begin with pastors behind the pulpit if there will ever be a change in the pews. New men and women are the only persons that can create a new world. New wine requires new containers. The new container represents a new person following salvation. It is the highest privilege given to believers to lend a helping hand and willing heart in this work of re-creation and restoration. With God in Christ, and Christ in us, we are able to go forth preaching and teaching, healing and helping by encouraging and inspiring in whose name we are called and with whom we serve.

Steps in Overcoming Spiritual Anemia

There are, of course, certain chronological steps that must be taken in order to deliver a person from the state of anemia. An anemic person must stop eating fast foods. The Hebrew people, because they belonged to God, were instructed what animals and herbs they were permitted to eat. Deuteronomy further listed the animals that were not permitted to be eaten. An old adage states, "We are what we eat." The proverb can be incorporated to include whatever we devote our attention

Chapter Six: An Analogy of Spiritual Anemia

too, we become. Society is urged to eat more wisely. (My question is: if the general population, as well as, the FDA and other governmental divisions understand certain foods in certain amounts are literally bad for prolonged consumption, why are they allowed to continue to be marketed as a consumer product? If government officials can band smoking and adult activities and literature until a certain age, and mandate seatbelts and helmets, etc., why not take harmful foods from the market place?)

Spiritual anemia is so rampant in society and in the average church particularly, the participants for change may have to wean a number of activities from their life while adopting a more nutritional diet. It will be most difficult to stop "cold turkey" because the anemic has grown an addiction to the affairs of the world. Lot's spirit became "vexed" while living in Sodom because he refused to leave the ungodly environment. (He kept *eating* [partaking and/or condoning] the same restaurants in his neighborhood. This is the reason God always instructed His saints to separate themselves from the ungodly.) As one develops a steady diet of reading the Bible (Colossians 3:16), a taste for prayer should increase. Changing restaurants (church) should begin the process of correcting the anemic problem. By refusing to eat the rich food from the kings table (Daniel 1:8-16), Daniel and his friends did not allow a weakened condition of anemia to occur. Moreover, God's diet allowed the four Hebrew boys to be more alert to their Chaldean instruction and more spiritually sensitive, which enabled Daniel to understand visions and dreams. In fact, Daniel and his friends were found to be ten times greater in health and wisdom than any other of the captives in Babylon.

I have presented the hypotheses that there is a growing presence of spiritual anemia among the Christian community. I defined spiritual anemia as a condition a Christian develops when he or she is not walking on a spiritual path or living a spiritual life as defined in Scripture. The supposition of anemia did not come from a conceited personality. Actually, the determining factor came from viewing the absence of spiritual fruit in the anemic person and/or churches. The reader has learned there is a developing "below par" standard among Christians when it comes to biblical knowledge and practice. I would like to expound further on the several possible causes of spiritual anemia in more detail followed by a few solutions to correct this condition that has been presented in this essay.

Chapter Six: An Analogy of Spiritual Anemia

First, there is a belief that church leadership, among a number of denominations, has not maintained a conservative theology. There is a belief among conservative Christians that such doctrinal truth is not considered as important today as it was at the turn of the century. The surrender of what is called hard preaching in the days gone by may be due from recent scientific discoveries or modern thought that has brought a neo-philosophy to public opinion. The resistance to keep the church informed of basic biblical doctrine over the years is believed to have brought about the spiritual anemic crisis in the 21st Century. Seminaries, pastors, and those who make up the average congregation have been deceived through the media, universities, and the scientific community with the belief man has now come of age – that he is no longer bound by metaphysical superstition. Thus, an amoral society has risen from the ashes of unbelief. With this unbelief comes the philosophy, via the current educational system and/or the lack there of found in the general church, that modern man does not need to obtain or maintain his standard of daily living from such an antiquated book known as the Bible or the belief in a God that is presented therein. If the Bible is out of date, sermons taken from the Bible must likewise have no real value to the current population.

Chapter Six: An Analogy of Spiritual Anemia

Contrary to belief, preaching on doctrinal subjects such as the inspiration of the Scripture, the Trinity, the Deity of Jesus, repentance, the church, or the second coming of Christ to name a few, should not be confused with the "fire and brimstone" messages of evangelism. There is a need for such messages similar to *Sinners in the Hand of a Living God*, by Jonathan Edwards; *Pay Day – Some Day*, by R. G. Lee; or *God's Three Dead Lines*, by J. Herald Smith. On the other hand, messages based on doctrinal or biblical content merely keeps the believer in every generation informed of the proper relationship a follower of God should have with his Creator. Scripture is filled with commands that show mankind how to walk before God.

Because lightning has not fallen in judgment nor has the earth opened to swallow those of unbelief for forsaking biblical instruction, the neo-Christian has developed less of a need for a Creator or Savior, and in so doing, will continue to distance himself from God. It is less important to the anemic to retain any substantial knowledge of God in the post-modern – high-tech world. Therefore, the sermons have become more shallow for the shallow-thinking Christian.

CHAPTER SIX: AN ANALOGY OF SPIRITUAL ANEMIA

Second, a number of Christian churches have abandoned serious biblical exposition and theological instruction. Teaching biblical doctrine has almost become a lost art. It takes study and a concentrated preparation to develop and write a sermon. Proper exegesis of any text can not be honestly delivered in a fifteen minute talk. This may be the reason many of today's congregations seem to be demanding more positive messages (e.g., Joel Osteen or Robert Schuler) rather than the ones calling for repentance or those proclaiming "Thus saith, the Lord God." There seems to be a demand for shorter sermons and for messages that will not cause a person to fall under conviction for wrong doing. But in the beginning, when Jerusalem heard Peter preach on the day of Pentecost, "...they were pricked in their heart and three thousand were saved" (Acts 2:37). In contrast, when Stephen preached (Acts 7: 54), the people were cut to the heart as they were at Pentecost but refused to repent. Rather, they bit Stephen with their teeth...they cried out with a loud voice, and stopped their ears, and ran upon him for the purpose of silencing the deacon. The rioters finally cast him out of the city and stoned him to death (verse 59). The anemic residents of Jerusalem did not wish to hear and/or accept Stephen's new faith even though it would have healed their spirits. Killing the deacon was the only

CHAPTER SIX: AN ANALOGY OF SPIRITUAL ANEMIA

way to silence what they believed to be sacrilege. The devil only succeeded in closing one door, but God was opening a larger and more powerful door in the Apostle Paul who witnessed the dreadful deed.

The third thing that concerns conservative Christians about preaching is the lack of practical application. Today's neo-pastors, unfamiliar with the literal interpretation, have a difficult time relating scripture to the daily needs and problems Christians are having. The neo-pastor is so far removed from what the Bible says and from what a person is suffering; he seemingly approaches the pulpit by rote to do his Sunday address.

Society has grown used to the fast service one finds at drive-up windows; people want everything to fit into a nice box without waiting. Americans have become accustomed to seeing 10 ounces of coffee and 12 ounces of bacon being substituted for the old 16-ounce pound. No church can expect to produce a strong Christian on a diet of fast food devotionals or sermons. The contemporary church wants to worship God on the run. The modernist no longer wishes to stand still and listen for the Spirit of God to speak personally to him or her out of fear He may suggest a life

CHAPTER SIX: AN ANALOGY OF SPIRITUAL ANEMIA

change and/or may fear God would present a commission to spread the gospel where neither no longer wished to go.

I have found it difficult to find another Christian (pastors included) willing, able, and knowledgeable enough to discuss biblical doctrine as it relates to current events. There have been two to three generations of Christians who grew up on sermonettes to substantiate the theory that people, young and old, do not wish to consider the signs of the times, or the root cause society is currently experiencing, and/or the ultimate outcome. Pastors who are caught up in a fast-paced ministry tend to find little time for serious theological discussions. Much of the religious literature, including the Sunday school lesson, has become shallow. There are a lot of pages of fill-in-the-blanks that make up the texts, but there is not enough spiritual meat for the believer to maintain strength enough to successfully contend for the faith. This becomes extremely important when one is experiencing spiritual warfare. (The average church member has never heard the term, "spiritual warfare," not alone the true meaning behind the phrase.) Literature for children has more activities that seem not to have anything to do with the lesson; and we wonder what has happened to the youth that were raised in church under such teaching and to the adults who have

CHAPTER SIX: AN ANALOGY OF SPIRITUAL ANEMIA

become engulfed in the world's temptations. Could it be the lack of true biblical teaching? (One needs only to compare today's Bible lessons with those 25 to 50 years ago.) We used to preach that God's word never changes; but something indeed must have changed. It is not only the methodology, but I submit over 60% of Bible content has been set aside as being too antiquated for this generation. The church seems to have adopted the same philosophy of the public educational system. Students are passed to the next grade level or allowed to graduate that cannot read or write. A thirty year old church member has never heard a series of lessons on the Patriarchs, the Tabernacle, the Ten Commandments, the Major and Minor Prophets, or the Importance of the Church. The same young adult shows no concern over current affairs because history and faith of our forefathers have been deleted from the curriculum. Matter of fact, the church should incorporate such a study into its teaching program. I am not saying we need to go back to the one room church or school with kerosene lamps. On the contrary, we should take advantage of modern technology, such as Power Point, to present God's word in a format that today's society can accept and understand.

There needs to be a stronger presentation of pure theological thought in our evangelical churches to ward off the tremendous influence of unbiblical and Eastern philosophies and erroneous worldviews that are steadily weakening the average church member. Liberal literary publications found on the American market continue to sew doubt about Jesus Christ, the Bible's authenticity, as well as the importance the church should have on society. A mere 32% of Christians believe in absolute truth. This leaves the church vulnerable to an array of demonic attacks and illnesses.

Phase 1 – *Determining the Extent of Spiritual Anemia*

The first step must begin with church leaders. Pastors and staff must recognize there is a spiritual crisis facing the church. Sadly, many pastors, rather than take the chance of rocking the boat (causing internal unrest), would rather preach their sermonettes to those who have grown to be Christianettes with the hope that some of the congregation manages to glean enough information to obtain some sort of salvation. The lack of doctrinal preaching is telling the present generation that God has changed the requirements of learning about Him.

The lack of simple biblical knowledge in the average congregation has caused some pastors recently to take a

CHAPTER SIX: AN ANALOGY OF SPIRITUAL ANEMIA

diagnostic survey of their own church to determine what the members actually believe. The survey must include everyone. If a deficiency of Bible knowledge is discovered, a plan must be developed speedily to correct the disease of anemia before it stagnates or destroys the church. The questionnaire should include basic Bible doctrine: is the Bible dependable and inerrant; is there salvation in any person or way other than Jesus Christ; was Jesus sinless, if so why; is there a real evil entity known as Satan, to name a few.

Good parents know their children and take an active part in their learning. Therefore, the parents must ask: what type of education are they receiving; what books are being read; what television shows or DVDs are being watched; what kind of music is being listened too? Pastors, who are God's under-shepherds, likewise, have the responsibility to look after the sheep, feed the flock, and protect his people from all heresies. A basic doctrinal class could be taught regularly or preached often. (Some churches require all staff, lay leaders, and deacons sign a statement of faith before assuming their positions.)

Society has been convinced, via a media blitz, of the idea that all foods should contain no sugar and be low in sodium. As many foods are literally stripped of their nutritional value, much of God's word on Sunday morning has been likewise stripped of its spiritual worth. Synthetic substitutes have been added to our food products to replace what has been deleted so the product *will appear* the same. Similarly, additives of psychology, Eastern philosophy, and liberalism or easy believeism etc., are replacing tested biblical doctrine. The absence of theology calls for a curriculum of systematic theology: we need to teach why we believe what we believe? There should be a course developed that teaches how great men and women retained their faith beginning with the church fathers and continue to include the faith of this century's leaders. There is a dire need to learn about men of prophetic power; spiritual warfare, and end times. These words remain unfamiliar, as I stated before, to scores of congregations. Pastors must alert their congregations to unbiblical doctrines and passing fads that will become destructive errors and heresies. A lesson series on Satan and demonism should become a major objective. I am glad to learn a number of America's mega churches are beginning to see the need to change back to a more biblical stance in their teaching. The course of action will be difficult, but very needful if the pastors are concerned enough for the salvation of the membership along with the future of this nation.

Finally, the teaching staff should be often encouraged. A temperament or gifted evaluation should be given to staff members and teachers; in fact, an in-depth Bible lesson of such should be made available for the whole congregation, especially new members within six months of them joining the church. Conservative biblical resources should be made available; a Christian library set up; and a knowledgeable speaker should be called to motivate the entire church including the leadership. Some people would call such a meeting a revival.

Phase 2 – Spiritual Solutions to Spiritual Anemia

There are several things a person can do in order to amend his or her health problems that relates to the body. First, admit there is a problem; second, submit to a physical examination to determine the exact area that is affected; third, develop a plan to help you follow the doctor's recommendation – change of diet, medication, and/or exercise. Since man is a trycodomy (body, soul, and spirit), he has a mind and soul that can become just as ill as his body. The most overlooked area that affects the body and mind is the spirit. (The thesis of this essay focuses on when the spiritual part of man becomes depleted of energy.) The same three procedures presented above to heal the body can

CHAPTER SIX: AN ANALOGY OF SPIRITUAL ANEMIA

likewise be used to heal the mind and spirit.

There was a period in time when the body was considered the only primary part of the human being that required medical attention. The pendulum has begun to swing back toward the center of reasoning, but it continues to be a slow process. Hindrances still exist. There are those who wish to treat man's different areas or parts as separate entities. Scientists believe the body belongs to the doctor, the mind to the psychiatrist, and the soul to the minister. The truth is that all three entities of man are interwoven, so much so, that each part affects one another. When a person is viewed as a *whole life*, a more complete healing can be accomplished. This is the reason the topic "spiritual anemia" was chosen. Once spiritual health is restored, the statistics are high enough to show the other parts of man can obtain a richer fulfillment. I believe most everyone has accepted the saying, "A person can make him or herself sick." There is medical proof an illness can develop without the presence of a virus or bacteria.

Unless the reader forgets, the subject of illness being discussed is spiritual anemia. The shortfall of spirituality is affecting every facet of life, not only the well-being of the church. I have tried to make the case among my peers that man himself is responsible for his failing spiritual health, even if he has not recognized his condition. I further believe in the person known as Satan or the devil. He is the chief adversary of the human race in all facets of living. The Apostle Paul warns us that our real battle is not with fellow humans, although the devil will use our peers and our own flesh against us. The correct sequence is: the Spirit over the mind; in other words, God's Spirit (in conjunction with our life-spirit) recommends to the mind what to think and do. The mind, in turn, tells the body what to do and what not to do. For example, when the flesh tells the mind that it wants preeminence, there will be trouble. Man should never think with his flesh, or he would never have enough cake and ice cream. The flesh will develop an unimaginable hunger that will become uncontrollable. We need the supernatural presence of the Holy Spirit. Paul said that the Christian is not wrestling with flesh and blood but against the rulers of darkness of this world, and against spiritual wickedness in high places. (Ephesians 6:12, paraphrased.) Consider the following equations: ***Incorrect***: body – mind – spirit; ***Incorrect*** New Age philosophy: mind/spirit – body; **Correct** biblical philosophy: Spirit – mind – body.

I have said that the fading of God from the lives of

CHAPTER SIX: AN ANALOGY OF SPIRITUAL ANEMIA

Christians has resulted in a growing epidemic among churches around the world, but especially in America. I came to this conclusion first by observing how the Christian community acted toward sin 20 or 30 years ago and how it accepts or overlooks the same sin today. I made note of the main emphasis of sermons during the same period and today. I have asked the older generation what was the general attitude in America toward deviate behavior? Has the reader determined there is a difference? What is the reason behind this difference? Do we not read the same Bible (possibly not); sin used to be sin. Has the reader noticed a growth in violence and its severity, and unspeakable mutilations? Has the reader noticed any change in ideas, philosophy, education, or politics in society in the last few years?

In the past, when society moved too quickly away from God, God's people used to pray for a correction. Corrections use to take place in the form of revivals. The only problem seemed to be that whatever correction was made never quite returned to center. More and more neo-philosophical ideas continued to infiltrate America from Europe and the Far East. These ideas soon found their way into the country's public schools and universities and court system. Thus, the institutions of learning produced more graduates that held a more liberal stance than the preceding generation (seminaries included). Before the biblical Christian realized what was happening, these concepts from the left found their way into the evangelical churches and more devastatingly into our political system. The philosophy of the far-left has taken the place of the supernatural spiritual God of the Bible. Consequently, foreign reasoning produced a moral decay which, in turn, caused God to begin fading from general believers, their churches, and their communities. In other words, America began going to pieces morally because her churches were going to pieces religiously.

We have accepted another gospel (Galatians 1:8); thus, we have lost the basis of morals and the ability to have close contact with or revelation from the Spirit of God. Unless a number of evangelicals are willing to move back toward God, like Jacob, and renew their former beliefs, the entire country is doomed as we know it.

More Christians and pastors are beginning to ask for spiritual refreshment. *If [you knew] the gift of God...[you] would have asked him and he would have given [you] living water* (John 4:10). A few individuals in this generation are finally waking up to the reality that they cannot live on

CHAPTER SIX: AN ANALOGY OF SPIRITUAL ANEMIA

illusions of reason or total science. Humanity was hardwired to have faith in the unseen. The writer of the Book of Hebrews said, *Now faith is the substance of the things hoped for, the evidence of things not seen* (Hebrews 11:1). A minister once said as he explained the doctrine of faith to his congregation, "Faith sees the invisible, believes the incredible, and receives the impossible."

Scientists have learned that dark energy and dark matter exists; in fact, dark energy comprises about 70% of the known cosmos, and dark matter makes up the other 25%. How do we know of its existence? Gravity! Gravity cannot be seen but we can see the effects it has on other heavenly bodies, and we can feel the pull of gravity upon our own bodies. What keeps everything balanced; what keeps the stars in place and the sun giving light? Those of us who are spiritual call that power, God, even though we are unable to see Him face-to-face. Most men admit there is something within them they are unable to explain, and there is something beyond their vision that remains a question. They further believe that all of existence needs the unseen power of creation or it will begin to crumble when mankind continues to deny the existence of the said power that governs creation. The spiritual anemic person has let go of that inner entity that was above him. Therefore, the anemic will continue to yield more of himself to that which is around him until there is nothing more to sustain him. Someone said that, "An atheist is a person who has no visible means of support."

I believe God will continue to fade from the minds and hearts of this age until all the teaching of doubt ceases from the universities, and until the court system begins to make better rulings based on right thinking, and the media stops promoting the left's agenda. "…Woe unto that [person] by whom [Jesus Christ] is betrayed: [or denied]" (Matthew 26:24).

Hope can be seen in the same people who once denied God's existence when they begin to rethink their former view. The change of thinking has revealed to society that it cannot live in harmony with others or with nature. The last generation is finding, to its surprise, that their denial of the truth that held their grandparent's existence together has begun to crumble under their feet. They found that their proclamation of nothing was in itself an illusion. This generation has realized that no foundation of being can be built with smoke and mirrors. The past generation has

CHAPTER SIX: AN ANALOGY OF SPIRITUAL ANEMIA

sneered at the Bible and the God of the Bible. The present generation is sneering at the people who believe in the God of the Bible and His church. They have learned too late that life cannot rest on nor have meaning based on nothing. The future of the world is in the hands of believers because the non believers have nothing within on which to act. Unbelievers are suffering from the paralysis of analyses; they can only deny.

Regrettably, the deniers who were responsible for several generations of doubters and those who rejected truth have nonetheless influenced the growth of spiritual anemia. The only way to correct the condition of anemia is to return to the Spirit of God and beg His forgiveness. The trip may be uphill, and the journey may be twice as difficult as before; but God is a loving God who offers a second chance. Recovery begins with the anemic admitting he or she needs help; more important, the anemic must want help before true healing can take place. The "want to" begins on the inside when the spiritual anemic turns from his pseudo religion and allows the inner will to tell the body: "What ever it takes, that is what I am going to do." The present generation needs the same desire Jacob had when he wrestled the Angel of the Lord. He held on until he received a blessing.

CHAPTER SIX: AN ANALOGY OF SPIRITUAL ANEMIA

The second step toward healing would require changing directions. Biblically, it is called repentance – the believer turning toward God from the world. The promise is, if a person draws near to God, then God will draw near to that person. The anemic may want change but is reluctant to follow through with what it would require to obtain change. (John Mark retreated from following Paul on the very first missionary journey due to his immature state.) There is the possibility the physically ill may not want to give up the fast foods, rich diets, or lazy living. He would rather remain a "couch potato." The spiritual anemic may be comfortable in a liberal church or no church at all, where the sermon or the lack there of, will not motivate him to change or to repent. Thus, he will continue feeding his soul with spiritual depleted nourishment until life's end. If the spiritual anemic truly desires change, it may take extra effort and time to locate a Bible preaching church. The spiritual anemic may also have to replace his or her former friends with those who are more spiritually mature. In fact, the more mature persons would make better friends in the long run. They would be more of an encouragement for him to remain on his corrected course. This goes for spiritual anemic pastors. They need to surround themselves or fellowship with like-minded men and women that rightly divide the word of truth.

CHAPTER SIX: AN ANALOGY OF SPIRITUAL ANEMIA

Once the spiritual anemic changes his mind by repenting, he has taken his first step toward returning to God. It is like the prodigal son in (Luke 15:11-20); "And when he came to himself" (mentally); "He arose and came to his father." The younger son retreated (repented) from the pigpen to the farm. The young man thought to himself that working on the farm as a servant would be better than wading in slop and mud.

We come now to the third step. The anemic should attune his steps through the eyes of Christ. By keeping his eyes upon Christ, the light of the world will *grow strangely dim*. The anemic should view himself through God's eyes. One should ask, "How does God see me?" The prodigal wanted to please the father. The wayward son left his rebellious attitude in the pigpen. When he first met his father on his return he said, "Make me as one of your servants"(v.9). The repentant anemic son did not finish his prepared speech. His father forgave his younger son as he hugged him and called for proper clothes, shoes, and a ring to be given to him before he arrived at the house so all could see that the son who had been lost has now returned home. (When the servants saw the shoes and ring on the youngest son, they realized that he had regained his position and authority in the family.) The son's attention was now upon his father and not on the temptations of the world that enticed him to leave home a few months earlier. With a new attitude in place, riches of the world did not matter any more. The praise of his former friends faded to the evident love and praise of his father.

We all should pray, "Lord, let me look through your eyes to see the truth." If we did, we would not be tempted like the Pharisee but rather have the temperament of the publican: "Forgive me, a worthless sinner." If we would keep our eyes upon Jesus, we would not be apt to sink into the sea of fear like Peter. If we would see through the eyes of Jesus, we would see, "The fields...white already to harvest," (John 4:35).

The repentant anemic, by turning back to God the Father, will be more likely to attend church more faithful; read God's word with a open heart and to pray more consistently. During this process, at some time, the believer will accept the fact, in faith, that the Heavenly Father has forgiven him by welcoming him back into the family as a son *with all rights, privileges, and honors pertain there of to his salvation*. Along the way the devil will tell the anemic son that he does not deserve to return to the fellowship of the

Chapter Six: An Analogy of Spiritual Anemia

saints as he reminds the son of all the good times he had in the past. The devil will try to use his former friends to tempt him back to his former life, even though he has been welcomed back with all the gifts and rejoicing.

The spiritual anemic, even in his repentant state, must be warned that he will not immediately feel necessarily at home in the church or feel like singing the old songs, etc., before total healing of his soul/spirit can take place. The lack of knowledge of this truth has brought defeat to scores of returning believers. It is like when a doctor gives a patient an injection of medication with the assurance it will make the patient feel better, but the patient will not realize the full effects of the medication until later. Likewise, the rejuvenating Christian may not feel as spiritually strong as other saints immediately. The fact that he has left the environment of the pigpen, and the temptations of the world, helps his soul receive the spiritual medication of preaching, reading, and praying. We all must remember that the devil will use the world to temp one back to him. The devil will try and use the flesh of the repentant saint, since it is still under the death warrant of Adam, even though the soul is saved and sealed for heaven (Ephesians 4:30). Since the devil will send distractions and temptations to the one that

Chapter Six: An Analogy of Spiritual Anemia

wants to correct his living, it is most important to encourage him to remain focused on the things and people that God has placed in his path to assist in his total spiritual makeover.

We who are helping the person return to God must be aware that the person may fail to respond as quickly as we would like. If it takes several weeks to recover from a major illness, it seems reasonable that it would require several months for a backslidden person to regain his lost spiritual yardage where he or she would once again enjoy God's salvation.

Finally, to continue one's spiritual renewal, and stay on the corrected path, you must develop a plan to be alone with God. Set aside time to read His word and to meditate on what has been read. Take walks (for physical health) and take notice of God's creation. Be sure to fellowship with like-believers and learn the meaning and purpose of the church, your talents, and spiritual gifts. By turning you back on the world and looking toward Jesus like Mary and Martha, be ready to listen rather than to talk. Your vision will improve, which will enable you to see the need of others. You will weep as Jesus wept and see sinners as He sees them. Soon you will see the sick healed and the lost saved and added to the church on a daily basis. Before long, without realizing it, the once anemic will become spiritual and will take his place in the harvesting of souls.

Brethren, if a man be overtaken in a fault, ye which are spiritual restore such a one in the spirit of meekness; considering thyself, lest thou also be tempted. Bear ye one another's burdens, and so fulfill the law of Christ, (Galatians 6:1-2).

Brethren, if any of you do err from the truth and one convert him; let him know that he which converteth the sinner from the error of his way shall save a soul from death, and shall hide a multitude of sins, (James 6: 19-20).

(Jesus speaking) *But I have prayed for thee, that they faith fail not; and when thou art converted, strengthen they brethren,* (Luke 22:32).

Notes:

CHAPTER SIX: AN ANALOGY OF SPIRITUAL ANEMIA

http://www.news.CrossWalk.com

http://www.georgebarna.org/FlexPage.aspx?Page=Barnaupdates

http://www.the-highway.com

http://www.preachingtoday.com

"Americans Draw Theological Beliefs from Divers Points of View," Oct. 2002
"Religious Beliefs Vary Widely By Denomination," June 25, 2001

Topics visited for reading:
General Christian Beliefs, Salvation, Bible, Theological Beliefs, & Satan.

APPENDIX

Sermon Outlines

HOLY HEARTBURN
Text: Luke 24:13-35

Introduction: Discuss the physical characteristics of a heartburn.
Setting: On the road to Emmaus.

I. Jesus joins the two travelers.
    A. Jesus begins teaching of Himself from the Scriptures.
    B. Jesus continues His fellowship.
    C. Jesus disappears following communion.
    D. The disciples realize who the traveler was.
II. What does the Word of God (Bible) mean to you?
    A. Viewed as the very Word of God.
        1. Inspired and Inerrant Document.
        2. Powerful and Living Document.
    B. Answers man's questions about God and himself.
III. How to develop a holy heartburn.
    A. Renew your love and commitment to God.
    B. Read the Bible on a daily basis.
    C. Rely on the Holy Spirit to guide you in the right direction and worship.
    D. Tell others about your salvation experience and what it means to you.

APPENDIX

LEAVING THE SAVIOR BEHIND
Text: Luke 2:41-50

Introduction: Discuss the origin of the Passover (Exodus 12:22) and the requirements to travel to Jerusalem once a year.

I. Jesus Was Left Behind in Jerusalem.
   A. Possible causes for leaving Jesus behind.
   B. The parents returned to Jerusalem.
     1. Back tracking and locating Jesus took three days.
     2. Jesus was found in the Temple talking to the Priests.
II. Have You Left Jesus Behind in Your Travels?
   A. From your daily activities?
   B. From your day of worship?

Conclusion: You may have to retrace your steps (life) in order to learn where you left Jesus standing alone. You have to ask yourself one question, "Do I truly want Jesus back into my life?"

THE PARABLE OF THE SOWER, SEEDS AND SOILS.
Text: Matthew 13:1-10

Introduction: Explain the characteristics of a parable, and the reason Jesus chose to teach by parables. Give the setting of the narrative and what or who the sower, seeds, and soils represent.

APPENDIX

I. Some Seed Fell on the Wayside.
   A. The term, "Wayside."
      1. The location of the wayside.
      2. The characteristic of the wayside area.
   B. The Seed Remained on the Surface.
      1. The Holy Spirit is hindered from working.
      2. The birds steal the seed.
II. Some Seed Fell Upon Stony Places.
   A. The characteristic of stony places.
      1. The characteristics of a "stony place" Christian.
      2. There is a process for clearing land before planting is possible.
   B. Rocks typify personal problems.
      1. Rocks can typify sin.
      2. Rocks can typify mental, emotional, and spiritual disorders.
      3. Rocks come in a variety of sizes.
         a. Some rocks lay on the surface.
         b. Other rocks lay below the surface.
   C. Rocks can be removed.
      1. Some rocks are easier to remove than others.
      2. Larger rocks may require more labor and commitment to remove.
      3. A few rocks may become "pet rocks" that you do not wish to give up.
      4. Rocks must be removed by the land owner.
   D. Rocks come with different names.
      1. The individual landowner must determine the

APPENDIX

   names.
   2. The Bible may assist the landowner in determining their names.
  E. The Sun becomes an adversary.
   1. There will be problems in life – there is no way to escape this truth.
   2. The devil will compound the problems to defeat the Christian.
   3. Jesus warns believers that they will suffer persecution.
III. Some Seeds Fell Among Thorns.
  A. Thorns or vines hinder the growth of the plant.
   1. The characteristics of a weedy area.
   2. Tares symbolize physical and spiritual hazards for the Christian.
   3. Tares present a greater hazard to the Christian testimony than the rocks.
  A. Tares can be sown on purpose by Satan.
   1. Christians are not exempt from problems or temptations.
   2. Tares can attack without warning.
   3. The mind becomes the proving or battle ground.
  C. Problems, people, and possessions can become tares in the devil's hand.
   1. The Christian must be aware of the possible growth of tares.
   2. The individual Christian is the only person able to deal with his tares.

APPENDIX

IV. Some Seeds Fell on Good Ground.
    A. Good ground was prepared to receive seed.
    B. Not all plants will produce the same amount of fruit.
    C. The Christian must learn how God works.
        1. He must learn how to deal with the weeds of life.
        2. He must understand God has set certain guidelines to follow.
        3. He must realize what power and what rights Christians have.

Conclusion: Christians must never stop watching for hazards that will disrupt their life. They must take responsibility of ownership of their garden. They must learn how to become mature in Spirit, as well as, how to battle that which will invade their space for the purpose of destroying or at least hindering future growth.

SLEEPING SAINTS

Introduction To Sleeping Saints.

I. Dead Saints Asleep in Christ.
II. Sleeping Saints are Carnal.
III. Sleeping Saints Are Insensitive to Sin.
IV. Sleeping Saints Are Unconcerned With Spiritual Matters.
V. Sleeping Saints Can Not Hear the Message of God.

APPENDIX

SLEEPING DURING PREACHING

Introduction: Christians need to wake up to the things of God.

I. Sleeping During Preaching.
    A. Spiritual Sleep.
        1. The Church at Ephesus.
        2. The Church at Smyrna.
        3. The Church at Pergomos.
        4. The Church at Thyatira.
        5. The Church at Sardis.
        6. The Church at Philadelphia.
        7. The Church at Laodicea.
    B. Satan's mist of sleep hinders the Christian influence.

SLEEPING DURING THE TRANSFIGURATION

I. Jesus Instructs Peter, James and John.
II. Jesus Physically Changes into His Glorified State.
III. The visit from the Lawmaker and Prophet proves a doctrinal point.
IV. The three Apostles sleep through the lesson.
    A. Peter's mistaken response.
    B. God the Father's rebuttal.

APPENDIX

SLEEPING DURING PRAYER

I. Sleeping During the Time of Prayer.
   A. Jesus requests for the Apostles to remain awake and to pray.
      1. Pray for spiritual strength for the Savior.
      2. Pray for spiritual strength for the Apostles against temptation.

II. The Church Needs Christians Praying.
   A. Pray for their Pastor.
   B. Pray for one another.
   C. Pray for the church's outreach into the community.

III. Sleeping While Danger Lurks.
   A. Time continues to past while the church sleeps.
   B. The devil continues his work while the church sleeps.

Conclusion: Sleeping does not generate faith, wisdom, strength, or knowledge in knowing how to contend for the faith.

SLEEPING WHILE THE LORD TARRIES HIS RETURN

Text: Matthew 25:1-5

Introduction: Recap the four prior messages. Present the next event to occur on God's timeline – His return for the church. Emphasize that the Christian should be busy adding to the Kingdom until that time. The Old Testament priests had no place to sit and do nothing.

APPENDIX

I. The church is sleeping as people continue to die without Christ.
   A. Evangelistic Work Is Lagging Behind.
      1. The Great Commission is given five times in Scripture.
      2. The Christian Church has become one of the slowest growing denominations in the world.
   B. Hell is a real place.
II. The Church Is Sleeping During the Time of Harvest.
   A. The church seems unconcerned about the fate of the present generation.
   B. The church is focused on herself.
   C. The church needs to devise strategies to evangelize while she still can.
III. The Church Is Sleeping While Christ Prepares Heaven for Her Arrival.
   A. He has been laboring for more than 2,000 years.
   B. He has postponed His return in order that more souls would be saved.
IV. Sleeping Saints Will Loose Their Awards at the Bema Seat.
   A. Proof in the Parable of Talents.
   B. Proof in the Parable the Ten Virgins.

Conclusion: Show that God does have a timeline: when Noah finished the Ark, the rain fell; when the angels delivered Lot and his family from Sodom, the fire fell. One day soon the trumpet will sound and the church will be caught up to heaven and the fire will fall during the Tribulation. Until then, Paul encourages the church to "Awaken to righteousness." (1 Corinthians 15:34)

SATISFYING MAN'S NATURAL AND SPIRITUAL NEEDS FOR BODY AND SOUL

PART ONE: Satisfying Man's Natural Needs for His Body.

Introduction: Present man as a trycodomy – body, soul, and spirit. Show the uniqueness and individuality of the three parts. Stress that Adam was patterned after his creator. Show the results of man's fall.

I. Man Needs Air to Breath.
II. Man Needs Water to Sustain Life.
III. Man Needs Rest or Sleep to Organize and Settle the Day's Activities.
IV. Man Needs to Understand His Emotional Need.
    A. He has a need for friendships with his fellow man.
    B. He has a need to maintain his motivational thrust.
    C. He has a need to be loved and to give love to another.

PART TWO: Satisfying Man's Spiritual Needs for His Soul.

Introduction: Revisit the individual characteristics of the Trinitarian God-Head. Re-enforce the aspect that man was created in the image of God. Discuss the relationship between God and man prior to and after man's fall. Show what sin is and what problems sin caused to their relationship. Show how God intervened to renew His relationship with mankind.

As God supplied the natural needs for the body, He has supplied, through Jesus Christ, like spiritual needs for the soul.

I. We would see Jesus for the Air of Eternal Life.
II. We would see Jesus for the Water of Life for Cleansing and Refreshing.
III. We would see Jesus for Spiritual Food to Strengthen and Nourish the Soul.
IV. We would see Jesus for Rest/Sleep – Bringing Peace to the Soul.
V. We would see Jesus for His Friendship Knowing We Will Never Have to Walk Alone.
VI. We Would See Jesus for Enough Ambition to Enable Us to Fulfill the Great Commission.
VII. We Would See Jesus for His Love to Enable Us to Love One Another – Even Those Who Are Not So Lovely.

Conclusion: Recap the needs for both – body and soul.

AN ANALOGY OF SPIRITUAL ANEMIA

Introduction: Discuss the characteristics of natural anemia. Present the thesis: There is a crisis among Christendom known as spiritual anemia.

APPENDIX

I. There Is a Crisis Facing Today's Church Viewed as a Spiritual Anemia.
   A. There is a "falling away" from knowing God.
      1. More emphasis is placed on the mechanics of growing a church than upon the Spirit adding to her ranks.
      2. Sermon content has been misdirected.
      3. Pastors approach their position as a job rather than a calling.
         a. Pastors tend to secure their positions by not "rocking the boat."
         b. Pastors tend to secure their positions by giving the congregation what they like to hear.
   B. Statistics show the lack of biblical knowledge is at an all-time low.
      1. Today's church members are unsure of the accuracy of the Bible.
      2. Today's church members are unsure of the deity of Jesus Christ. They do not understand the importance of this bedrock doctrine.
      3. Today's church members are unsure of the reality of Satan.
      4. Today's church members are unsure of the reality of the return of Christ.
   C. Maintaining a Christian philosophy is fading among believers.
II. What Caused the Present Anemic Condition Among Christians?

APPENDIX

A. Society has greatly influenced the church.
  1. No time is given to study or to meditate on God.
  2. We have been distracted with worldly living.
  3. We have developed a philosophy that everything should be accomplished instantly with little thought or work.

B. Liberal Education has greatly influenced the church.
  1. America's original institutions of higher learning were founded for the sole purpose of producing pastors.
  2. Religious curriculum has been replaced with a more secular friendly instruction.
  3. Liberal universities have produced liberal teachers and judges who are influencing a large percentage of the population.

III. God Has Not Given Up on This Generation.

A. There is a fresh burden for revival coming upon a number of God's ministers.
  1. A call for revival is being heard throughout the nation.
  2. A call for prayer is being heard throughout the nation.
  3. A call for repentance is being heard throughout the nation.

B. Pastors and Evangelists must begin preaching for change.

APPENDIX

IV. Steps For Overcoming Spiritual Anemia Must Be Developed.
    A. Diagnostic survey must be developed to determine the extent of the spiritual anemic condition.
    B. Sermons should address the present crisis of spiritual anemia.
    C. Pastors and Evangelists must reintroduce and show the importance of doctrine and theologies to the congregation.
        1. Develop a series of messages from "yesteryear" (giants of the faith).
        2. Show the characteristics of society prior to the two great revivals and parallel them to the present.
        3. Show the church, from God's word, the need to develop and grow spiritual.

    D. The church must be shown:
        1. Their need for change.
        2. Their need to change their ideology.
        3. Their need to change their worldly diet to a more spiritual balance.
        4. Their need to become more involved in the ministry.
        5. Their need to develop a quiet time to be with God.

APPENDIX

Conclusion:

Close by giving positive illustrations where God has move mightily. List what other ministries have done. Ask for commitment and show that time is racing by; the rapture is the next event on God's timeline. Inquire of the congregation's readiness.

About the Author

Rev. William Combs, Ph.D., began his biblical training in systematic theology with a minor in psychology and art. Following his Th.M. degree he added a Doctor of Philosophy in Religion. Over the years he has served as a pastor, evangelist, minister of education, and schoolteacher. He and his wife, Vera, live in Naples, Florida where he continues to be involved in the local church and local school system. He is available to hold conferences and revivals to relieve and encourage the suffering Christian sitting in the pew.

INDEX

Abraham 44, 96, 146, 257, 258
Adam 23, 47, 49, 66, 76, 77, 145, 191, 209, 210, 212, 216, 240, 241, 295, 308
ADD (Attention Deficient Disorder) 255
American courts 74
Anxiety 30
Apollo 47
Babylon 43, 259, 274
Behavior therapy 315
Blood 18, 33
Booth, Anna 234
Christian counselors 315
Cognitive therapy 315
Couch grass 315
Critics 41, 315
Daniel 6, 11, 43, 259, 273, 274
David 13, 36, 82, 84, 98, 147, 176, 200, 224, 238, 263, 264, 271, 272
Devil 66, 73, 86, 91, 95, 160
Emotion 193
Faith 33, 85, 101, 289
Fire 135
Forgiveness 29
Gideon 95, 96, 247
Grace 220
Green, Oliver, B. 238
Guilt 100
Heartburn 1, 2, 3, 4, 5, 6, 7, 8, 9, 10, 11, 12, 13, 14, 15, 16
Hell 153, 169, 171, 172, 307
Holy Spirit 8, 15, 25, 36, 37, 40, 43, 45

Hutson, Dr. Curtis 169
Jeremiah 6, 14, 42, 64, 176
Jerry B. Jenkins 33
Judgment 110, 163, 175
Lamb's Book of Life 15, 32
Laodicean Era 241
Lazarus 146, 216
Liberal 281, 311
Love 27, 66, 231, 233, 309
Mercy 147, 263
Motivation 89, 94, 202, 203, 204, 228, 229, 230, 231
Mullen, Dr. Wendell D. 232
Nebuchadnezzar 43, 259
Nicodemus 37, 92, 191
Noah 41, 42, 177, 263, 307
Nouthetic Counseling 52
OCD 51, 54
Oliver B. Green 220
Paradise 191
Passover 3, 17, 18, 26, 301
Paul Lee Tan 8, 9, 12
Pennell, Dr. Bill 234
Pharisees 129, 156, 190, 226
Post, Stephen, G. 232
Power Drinks 268
Pray 306
Psychiatrist 58, 285
Psychotherapy 56
Psychologist 58
Revival 259

Sadducees 41
Salvation 32, 170, 194, 212, 217, 235, 240, 298
Sanhedrin 41
Secular 58
Seed 39, 45, 302

INDEX

Sin 5, 49, 113, 144, 193, 194, 210, 212, 304
Stony Places 45, 302
Suicide 58, 154, 176, 225
Talents 307
Temple 5, 30, 31, 222, 301
Temptation 142
Ten Commandments 30, 74, 162, 256, 265, 266, 280
Thor's Hammer 64
Transfiguration 137, 139
Tree of Knowledge 191
Tribulation 25, 171, 178, 308
U.S. Constitution 265
Wayside 39, 302
Zig Zigler 229

SCRIPTURE INDEX

Chapter 1
2 Kings 7:5-9 15
Jeremiah 6, 14
Luke 24 1, 14
Luke 24: 13-35 1

Chapter 2
James 4:4 27

Chapter 3
1 Corinthians 1:4 60
1 John 2:15-17 66
1 Samuel 3:1-10 50
1 Samuel 18:10-12 55
1 Timothy 1:7 59
2 Corinthians 1:8b 60
2 Corinthians 10:5 57
2 Corinthians 11:14-15 84
2 Peter 3:7 66
2 Timothy 3:8 74
Acts 5:3 82
Acts 7:54 42
Ephesians 4:4-6
Ephesians 4:30 81
Ephesians 6:18 67
Exodus 17:10-12 67
Galatians 5:22 93, 98
Genesis 11:6-9 97
Genesis 15:11 44
Isaiah 5:1-2 61
James 1:14 65, 79
Jeremiah 23:29 64
Philippians 1:6 59
Proverbs 23:7 57
Revelation 18:2 43
Romans 1:28 40
Romans 5:12 66, 71
Romans 6:23 82
Romans 12:6 93

Chapter 4
1 Corinthians 15:34 168
1 Peter 2:2 112
1 Peter 5:8 161
Acts 8:30-31 172
Acts 20:6-12 121
Ephesians 2:8 47, 93, 148
Ephesians 5:14 181
Exodus 17:10-12 67, 158
Ezekiel 6:11 122
Galatians 2:16 148

SCRIPTURE INDEX

Hebrews 7:25 167
Hebrews 10:31 136
Isaiah 11:11 160
James 4:7 114
John 3:14 144
John 4:35 176, 294
Luke 11:24-26 160
Luke 12:49 142
Mark 9:26 160
Mathew 25:1-5 165
Proverbs 10:5 176
Proverbs 11:30 169
Revelation 2:1-3:22 126
Revelation 3:14-22 132, 241
Romans 8:34 167
Romans 13:11-14 113

Chapter 5
1 Corinthians 10:4 220
1 Corinthians 11:7 189
1 John 5:7 209
1 Peter 2:2 223
2 Corinthians 5:1-3 187
Colossians 3:10 189
Ecclesiastes 3:1-8 200
Ephesians 2:8 47, 93, 148, 212
Ephesians 4:4-6 209
Ephesians 4:30 81, 215, 217, 295
Ephesians 5:2 234
Exodus 20:3 218
Genesis 1:26-27 188, 212
Hebrews 4:12 183, 185
James 4:8 221, 261
John 1:12 220
John 3:3-7 210
John 3:16 212, 231

John 4:14 219
John 4:35 176, 294
John 10:28 214
John 11:25 216
John 12:20-21 183, 207
John 14:6 172, 240
John 14:17, 23 214
John 20:22 216
Romans 5:12 191, 210
Romans 8:5-12 183, 184
Romans 8:29 189

Chapter 6
1 Kings 11:2 264
2 Timothy 3:2-7 242
2 Timothy 4:3-4 247
Colossians 3:16 273
Ephesians 4:30 81, 215, 217, 295
Ephesians 6:12 286
Galatians 1:8 288
Galatians 6:1-2 297
Genesis 9:4 240
Hebrews 11:1 289
Isaiah 29:13 262
James 4:8 221, 261
John 4:10 288
John 3:16 212, 231
Leviticus 17:14 240
Luke 5:16 256
Luke 15:11-20 293
Luke 22:32 297
Proverbs 14:34 264
Psalms 9:17 264
Revelation 2:5 263
Revelation 3:14-22 132, 24
Romans 1:8 264

AUTHORS

Barna, George 249
Benner, David, G. 238
Carbonell, Mells 238
Carrington, W.L. 204
Collins, John 176
Wyne Dryer 203
Edwards, Jonathan 276
Green, Oliver, B. 220
Jenkins, Jerry B. 33
LaHaye, Tim 25, 33, 85, 101
Mete, Dr. Gabor 80
Meyer, Joyce 85, 101
Peterson, John W. 33
Smith, J. Herald 276
Strauss, Richard, L. 85, 101
Tan, Paul Lee 8, 9, 12
Thiessen, Henry, C. 238
Vine, W.E. 119
Dr. Charles Weigle 11

Made in the USA
Charleston, SC
06 August 2011